HALLIWELL'S
FILM QUIZ BOOK

ALSO AVAILABLE

Halliwell's Film & Video Guide 2001
Halliwell's Who's Who in the Movies

HALLIWELL'S FILM QUIZ BOOK

Andrew Murray

Edited by John Walker

 HarperCollins*Entertainment*
An Imprint of HarperCollins*Publishers*

HarperCollins*Entertainment*
An Imprint of HarperCollins*Publishers*
77–85 Fulham Palace Road,
Hammersmith, London W6 8JB

www.**fire**and**water**.com

A Paperback Original 2000
9 8 7 6 5 4 3 2 1

Copyright © Andrew Murray 2000
Foreword © John Walker 2000

The Author asserts the moral right to
be identified as the author of this work

A catalogue record for this book
is available from the British Library

ISBN 0 00 653194 6

Set in Futura

Printed and bound in Great Britain by
Omnia Books Limited, Glasgow

CONTENTS

INTRODUCTION

The twentieth century belonged to America, to the media and to celluloid. In the twenty-first century, George Lucas tells us to prepare to bid farewell to the latter. Sprocketed reels will soon be going to the grave, and feature films will be recorded on digital media, similar to how a PC stores information.

As the machines behind the screens are overhauled once again, it's too easy to think of film as a mechanical process, with films rolling off a Hollywood production line – Hollywood at its most humdrum, with pumping soundtracks telling you how to feel and plot formulas to set your watch by. Yet the reality is that the art of film-making is as creative as ever. Beyond the changing tools of film-making, the art remains: the imagination, the good ideas, and the daring to show us something that is different and valuable. *The Halliwell's Film Quiz Book* lets you dip your toe in a number of other cinematic waters – the films of Satyajit Ray and the Brothers Quay, strange animations, half-forgotten masters and rarely-seen treasures.

Alongside the wellsprings of fine film-making that still defiantly bubble up from Tinseltown, there is also the tingle of some refreshingly different currents. The few really special movies – the films that stretch your mind and heart into slightly different shapes – make cinema matter. Cinema is an art form and it is fun. The clear and authoritative voice of *Halliwell's Film & Video Guide* and *Halliwell's Who's Who in the Movies* covers the cinema of the world in depth. But where the Halliwell's guides wisely settle filmic arguments, the *Film Quiz* hopes to spark some.

In each themed section there is an ⑤ for Starter question, a main body of twelve questions, a ★ question for Connoisseurs and a **TB** Tiebreaker. Inevitably you will sometimes find the Connoisseur question easier than the Starter – such is life, and cinema!

Andrew Murray

FOREWORD

This book of quizzes covers every era of movie watching: from its earliest, novelty beginnings, through many of the greatest directors and stars to present-day talents such as Quentin Tarantino and the quirky Coen Brothers. It will remind you of many of the glories of Hollywood, as well as that there is more to cinema than Hollywood can provide. It will nudge your recall of yesterday's classics as well as of today's hits.

There is always fun to be had from matching your wits against a clever opponent. You can even enjoy watching a contest of brainpower: it's the underlying fascination of the James Bond movies, or of thrillers such as *The Thomas Crown Affair*, which was first made thirty-two years ago and recently re-made because of the enduring appeal of its central duel.

Within these pages, you'll have the satisfaction of testing your cinematic knowledge against a mind so devious that Dr No would have said yes to it. The questions will intrigue, stimulate and, probably, infuriate you. But, as the answers are at the back of the book, you'll also be painlessly informed about the twentieth century's greatest means of art and entertainment.

Like Helen Hayes's Dowager Empress in *Anastasia*, you can play solitaire with your memories, relishing its challenging questions on your own. But, with others, you can pursue with greater pleasure what may be trivia, but which will provide plenty of present amusement and stir remembrances of past delight.

Whatever. Enjoy!

John Walker

[1]
FOUNDING FATHERS

(S) Who said:
'Young man, you can be grateful that my invention is not for sale, for it would undoubtedly ruin you. It can be exploited for a certain time as a scientific curiosity, but apart from that it has no commercial value whatsoever'?

1   Did Pierre Janssen invent in 1874 a camera with a revolving photographic plate (a) to document the ceremony ending the Franco-Prussian War, (b) to record Venus passing across the sun, or (c) to photograph his daughter's wedding?

2   Why did Eadweard Muybridge stretch many lengths of thread across a track?

3   Where does the word 'cinema' come from?

4   What year was it when Louis Lumière first showed *Workers Leaving the Lumière Factory*?

5   Which famous Lumière short made spectators scream and duck?

6   What name was given to the primitive moving sound and light shows that preceded true cinema?

7   What is a pan, and where does the term come from?

8   When the Lumière operators toured the world, what were they instructed not to reveal, not even to kings and beautiful women?

9   Which company invented celluloid?

10 Which US President was impersonated in a bogus 1907 safari pic titled *Hunting Big Game* in Africa?

11 What was the general reaction of the world's royalty to the arrival of the Lumière operators?

12 For what physical reason did the world buy into the Lumière cinématographe rather than Thomas Edison's rival camera?

★   What was the rival term for cinema that Skladonowsky used in Germany?

TB Who was the magician who turned up at the Lumières' first screening, and tried vainly to buy a cinématographe there and then?

[2]
CHARLIE CHAPLIN

(5) Who did Jack Oakie play to Chaplin's Hitler (Adenoid Hynkel) in *The Great Dictator*?

1 Did Chaplin grow up in Ladywell, Lewisham, Leytonstone or Lambeth?

2 What do Chaplin and Mack Swain turn into a thanksgiving banquet in *The Gold Rush*?

3 And how does the hallucinating Swain see Chaplin?

4 *The Kid*. Uncle Fester in *The Addams Family*. The actor?

5 Chaplin (as well as Stan Laurel) sailed to America as a member of which impresario's troupe?

6 When Mack Sennett hired Chaplin, what were the names of his studio and of his most famous players?

7 To which committee did Chaplin describe himself as a 'peacemonger'?

8 Who played Chaplin's ballerina muse in *Limelight*?

9 'In the cold, dank climate of England, wearing his traditional loin-cloth, which he gathered about him in disorderly fashion, he seemed incongruous.' Who is Chaplin describing?

10 What is Chaplin's only concession to dialogue in *Modern Times*?

11 How did *The Kid* help Chaplin's Tramp drum up business?

12 In *The Cure*, what went wrong with the spa water meant to treat Chaplin's dipsomaniac?

★ In his 1947 film, who marries and murders a string of women to support his real wife?

TB What links Chaplin to *Doctor Zhivago*?

[3]
DIRECTING

(5) 'I didn't think the old man would bleed so much ...' Which impish director, reputedly speaking on a crowded lift?

1 Is the producer normally the employee of the director, or *vice-versa*?

2 Who gave the world the archetype of the director as monocled Teutonic autocrat?

3 How did the Philippines government muck up one of Francis Ford Coppola's shots of massed helicopters in *Apocalypse Now*?

4 Which actor-director directed a film about a director directing the actor who he also directed in *The Maltese Falcon*?

5 Who, during his long decline, complained 'When you're down and out, something always turns up – usually the noses of your friends'?

6 How did Alfred Hitchcock manage to put in his customary appearance within the confines of *Rope*?

7 Who reputedly cried 'Bring on the empty horses!'?

8 Name the director who links a river that don't go to Antry, an invisible people and a Blitz family who don't trust German jam.

9 Who reputedly insisted on nearly a hundred takes of Tom Cruise walking through a doorway?

10 What is *mise-en-scène*?

11 Which cut from Michael Powell's *A Canterbury Tale* inspired the bone to spaceship cut in *2001: A Space Odyssey*?

12 In *Walkabout*, Nicolas Roeg turns a sunset into what emblem?

★ What is the argument behind auteurism?

TB Who is so fond of filming rain that he even managed to get a shower into a spaceship?

[4]
ORSON WELLES

(5) Who or what was the immortal Rosebud?

1 On which media magnate's life was *Citizen Kane* based?

2 What was the place, and what was the time, that we met Harry Lime?

3 What theatre troupe did the boy wonder Welles bring with him to Hollywood?

4 Which Conrad novel was Welles only able to produce a few shots for, and had to wait another forty years for a Hollywood interpretation that did it any justice?

5 Which Welles tale begins with a single, suspenseful take of a figure planting a car bomb?

6 What was Welles's second feature, again with Mercury stalwarts like Joseph Cotten and Agnes Moorhead, and which still glitters despite studio interference?

7 What radio series of 1937 terrorised America with its apparently authentic news bulletins?

8 Is *Journey Into Fear* the tale (a) of a weapons engineer threatened by assassins in Istanbul, (b) of a Mexican drugs cop caught up in a border town murder, or (c) of a magical plot to produce a stand-in for Marie Antoinette?

9 Anthony Perkins as Joseph K. Jeanne Moreau. Welles as director and editor. An adaptation of what dark novel, by whom?

10 What ended with a shoot-out in a hall of mirrors?

11 If Paul Schofield is Thomas More, and Robert Shaw Henry VIII, then who is Welles?

12 Which studio produced *Kane*, and co-produced *The Magnificent Ambersons* with Mercury?

★ Which Alan Resnais film mimicked *Kane*'s opening shots of fences and warning notice?

TB Who co-wrote *Kane* with Welles, and fumed, 'There but for the grace of God, goes God'?

4

[5]
GERMAN CINEMA

(S) What city had a good Maria and a metal Maria?

1 'This story of a man and his wife is of nowhere, you might hear it anywhere and at any time.' The 1927 film?

2 Which Wolfgang Petersen epic had the inevitable liberal Captain and *Mein Kampf*-reading fanatic subordinate?

3 Was Wim Wenders's *Wings of Desire* about (a) Hitler's flight to a Nuremberg rally, (b) an angel who falls in love with a circus performer, or (c) a Conquistador party descending a river by raft?

4 Which Volker Schlöndorff film starred a boy who refused to grow up?

5 Max Schreck and Klaus Kinski have both played which nightmarish character?

6 German film production was galvanised by the formation in 1917 of what major company?

7 Who brought a grand visual style to thirties films like *The Blue Angel* and *The Scarlet Empress*?

8 Who became a major star with *The Blue Angel*?

9 Why was the Irishman trying to lift a riverboat over a mountain called *Fitzcarraldo*?

10 How long, to the nearest hour, did Erich von Stroheim's original version of *Greed* run?

11 Who directed *Olympische Spiele*, a bravura account of the 1936 Berlin Olympics, with worrying overtones?

12 *Berlin Alexanderplatz. Mother Kusters Goes to Heaven. The Marriage of Maria Braun.* The director?

★ What kind of film-making is Hans Richter best known for?

TB What home takes over fifteen hours to view?

[6]
KATHARINE HEPBURN

(S) Who or what was the baby in *Bringing Up Baby*?

1 'Nature, Mr Allnut, is ...' What?

2 Aside from her dull groom-to-be, who does Tracy Lord have to choose between in *The Philadelphia Story*?

3 Who came into Hepburn's life with *Woman of the Year*?

4 How was she famously branded by a major exhibitor: as Oscar poison, box office poison, or poison for the soul?

5 Name three of the four films for which Hepburn won Oscars.

6 How did Hepburn and Bogart intend to sink a German steamship on Lake Victoria?

7 What is the professional rivalry between Hepburn and Tracy in *Adam's Rib*?

8 Who did Hepburn play in *The Lion in Winter*: Catherine of Aragon, Eleanor of Aquitaine, or Mary Queen of Scots?

9 Who played her husband and daughter in *On Golden Pond*?

10 According to Dorothy Parker, Hepburn's acting ran what gamut of emotions?

11 In an adaptation of which Eugene O'Neill play did she play the matriarch of the troubled Tyrone family?

12 Why are the snobbish Hepburn and Tracy unhappy with their daughter in *Guess Who's Coming to Dinner*?

★ What did Robert Hopkins say of Hepburn's physical angularity?

TB Which of the Barrymore clan played Hepburn's father in *A Bill of Divorcement*?

[7]
FILM AND POLITICS

⑤ What does Forrest Gump report to the police from a Washington hotel?

1 Who were the Watergate reporters played by Robert Redford and Dustin Hoffman in *All the President's Men*?

2 Who, in a dark car park, gives Redford some of his most important clues?

3 In which conflict was Ken Loach's *Land and Freedom* set?

4 Which British director of TV films made *Contact*, about border patrols in Northern Ireland, and *Made in Britain*, about a skinhead?

5 And who played the skinhead?

6 Which 1968 film, co-directed by and starring John Wayne, was one of the very few Hollywood movies all in favour of the Vietnam War?

7 Which notorious Teamster boss was played by Sylvester Stallone in *F.I.S.T.*?

8 Who admitted to Communist affiliations to the House Un-American Activities Committee, before playing the Red-phobic General Jack D. Ripper in *Doctor Stangelove*?

9 Why was James Mason's Johnny dying in *Odd Man Out*?

10 Who was John Hinckley trying to impress when he shot President Reagan?

11 Who was *Bob Roberts*, a far-right, folk-singing Presidential candidate?

12 Who directed *All the President's Men* and *The Parallax View*, the one specifically about Watergate and the other infused with the mistrust of the establishment of the post-Watergate period?

★ What Government position did John Profumo hold before being forced to resign, as played by Ian McKellen in *Scandal*?

TB Who played Nixon in Oliver Stone's biopic?

[8]
2001: A SPACE ODYSSEY

(S) To what piece of music do the spaceship and docking station famously waltz early in *2001*?

1   Who moved on from portraying humanity at the mercy of nuclear weapons, in *Dr Strangelove*, to this vision of Man dwarfed by technology and space?

2   What object links the primeval, futuristic and mystical sections of the film?

3   What is the profound breakthrough made by the ape-man?

4   On what Arthur C. Clarke story is the film based?

5   Where was the Moon monolith sending its signals?

6   Who or what came to life in Urbana, Illinois, on 12 January 1992?

7   How did HAL know that Dave and Frank had decided in the sound-proofed pod to shut him down?

8   What slogan from the film *Alien* applies to the presentation of sound in *2001*, unlike most other sci-fi movies?

9   Why did the other crew-members never wake up?

10 Who moved on from the special effects of *2001* to work on *Close Encounters of the Third Kind*?

11 What did HAL sing as Dave shut him down?

12 What do you have to do to the initials HAL to come up with the name of a certain computer company?

★   What does HAL stand for?

TB Who recorded a glam-rock coda to *2001* with his Spiders from Mars?

[9]
HUMPHREY BOGART

⑤ Who *didn't* say, 'Play it again, Sam'?

1 'When you're slapped, you'll take it and like it!' Which film?

2 What era was it when rival mobsters Bogart and James Cagney went head to head?

3 Why the stiff upper lip?

4 Who was the sizeable villain who slipped Sam Spade a mickey?

5 Bogart got his first substantial screen role as gangster Duke Mantee, with Leslie Howard and Bette Davis, in which 1936 movie?

6 What loot did Bogart, Walter Huston and Tim Holt fall out over in a loose reworking of *The Pardoner's Tale*?

7 If Spade didn't exactly believe Miss O'Shea's story, what did he believe?

8 Adapted by William Faulkner, among others, from Raymond Chandler's novel. Directed by Howard Hawks. Bogart as Marlowe. Bacall steaming up the screen. Which *film noir*?

9 What did Rick have in *Casablanca* that was of such vital importance to Ingrid Bergman, and many others?

10 Where did Bogart have to contend with a hurricane, Lionel Barrymore, and a crazed Edward G. Robinson?

11 Who demonstrated how to run a ship by getting hysterical over some missing strawberries?

12 Which inimitable actor, clamouring for Rick's ticket out of Europe, in real life escaped rising anti-Semitism in Germany and his native Hungary?

★ Who progressed from being *Caligari*'s monster to Bogart's nemesis in *Casablanca*?

TB Who told Bogart, 'If you want anything, just whistle', whereupon in real life he wanted to marry her?

[10]
FRENCH CINEMA

(S) Which glossy French thriller of 1990 was remade by Hollywood as *The Assassin*?

1 What depiction of the theatreland of 1840s Paris was made within the constraints of the German occupation?

2 Who starred in it as the *pantomime* who falls in love with the unattainable Garance?

3 What film boasted a 25-minute robbery sequence carried out in silence?

4 Why did a pair of contact lenses give Vera Clouzot a heart attack in *Les Diaboliques*?

5 Who deftly directed many light comedies of the thirties, including *Le Million*, about a search for a lost lottery ticket?

6 What name was given to the iconoclastic group of young French directors, including Jean-Luc Godard and François Truffaut, who found fame in the early sixties?

7 Which director played the (very) stiff-necked POW camp commandant in Jean Renoir's anti-war film *La Grande Illusion*?

8 Which of Renoir's films charted the foibles and intrigues of the French aristocracy between the wars?

9 Who directed *L'Orphée*, a dreamlike fantasy based on the legend of Orpheus and Eurydice?

10 Why was the truck journey undertaken by Yves Montand and Charles Vanel in *The Wages of Fear* (*Le Salaire de la Peur*) so fearful?

11 Which facially-challenged soldier-poet was subtitled for Anglophone audiences with rhyming couplets by Anthony Burgess?

12 Whose light visual comedies included *Monsieur Hulot's Holiday*, *Mon Oncle* and *Jour de Fête*?

★ Which Alan Resnais film teased the viewer as to whether a man and a woman had had an affair the year before?

TB What was the name of Paris's theatre street in *Les Enfants du Paradis*?

[11]
COMEDY

(5) Who are Larry, Curly and Mo?

1   What two things happened if the phone rang when Inspector Clouseau and Cato were fighting?

2   Which director did Mel Brooks spoof in *High Anxiety*?

3   *Always look on the bright side of life* ...Whose life?

4   Groucho, Chico and Harpo we know, but name two other Marx Brothers

5   Who was born Leslie Townes in Eltham, south-east London?

6   *The Milky Way, Quiet Please* and *The Little Orphan*. The cartoon duo?

7   What was the shock tactic of the 'Devils in Skirts' in *Carry on up the Khyber*?

8   In which film does Cameron Diaz use a hair gel formula not recommended by the pharmacist?

9   ' ... And don't call me Shirley.' The 1980 movie?

10 Who saw a pentacle drawn in blood in a Yorkshire pub, and thought the owner might be from Texas?

11 How did Pat O'Brien react when Jack Lemmon told him he wasn't a woman after all?

12 Who was Bugs Bunny's Elegant Mess spoofing?

★   Who was the young girl Alec Guinness gave some money to so she could buy a gift at the beginning of *The Lavender Hill Mob*?

TB Which rock band had volume knobs that went up to 11?

[12]

STEVEN SPIELBERG

(S) Why did Indiana Smith become Indiana Jones?

1 What shape did Richard Dreyfus try to recreate in sketch, mud and shaving foam in *Close Encounters of the Third Kind*, and why?

2 What kind of dinosaurs stalked the children through the kitchens in *Jurassic Park*?

3 Which gripping TV movie of a motorist terrorised by a demon truck showed that the young Spielberg had studied his Hitchcock, but also that his own style was coming to fruition?

4 What is a Carcharodon carcharias?

5 And who accompanied Roy Scheider in an under-specified tub to kill it?

6 If 1993 marked Spielberg's return to the box-office record breaker with *Jurassic Park*, how did it mark a kind of coming of age as a director?

7 In which Spielberg movie did friend George Lucas find a nice product placement for his Snaggletooth, Greedo and Hammerhead figures?

8 What year was it when Dan Aykroyd and Mickey Rourke sweated in the same tank, and Toshiro Mifune, as ever, provided Hollywood's idea of the Yellow Peril?

9 An Alice Walker novel. Whoopi Goldberg, Oprah Winfrey and Danny Glover. What was the hue of Spielberg's first attempt at something more than crash-bang-wallop?

10 J. G. Ballard's recollections of his time in a Japanese internment camp during the War became which film?

11 Which outing, with Spielberg as Executive Producer, had an unlikely teenager solving unlikely dilemmas in a very unlikely choice of time-travel vehicle?

12 Who was a peripheral, if charismatic, presence in *Jurassic Park* but starred, a blockbuster boffin for all seasons, in *The Lost World*?

★ Which great film of the previous year influenced *Sugarland Express* in its tale of the trail of mayhem aimlessly left by a young couple?

TB Aged 15, Spielberg directed a mini-epic, *Firestorm*, on a $3000 budget, and had it screened at three local cinemas. True or false?

[13]
ANIMATORS

(S) Name the model animation technique used in the Wallace and Gromit films.

1 What was the name of the cartoon character that Winsor McKay introduced to the world in 1909?

2 Who created Droopy among his sassy, brilliantly timed cartoons?

3 Which Czech animator satirised state repression in *The Glove*, and went on to produce macabre versions of *Alice in Wonderland* and *Faust*?

4 Who appealed to Eddie Valiant for help after being framed by a villain from Toon Town?

5 Which film features a mayor with two faces and a spider for a tie, a scientist with a flip-top head, and Jack Skellington, the Pumpkin King?

6 Who often drew his animations directly onto the celluloid, as in *Hen Hop*?

7 Nick Park won two Oscars with Wallace and Gromit, but which film won him his first statuette?

8 Which National Film Board is of particular note for sponsoring animators, including Norman McLaren and Richard Williams?

9 *Flowers and Trees*, *The Three Caballeros*, *Dr Syn*, *Son of Flubber*. The producer?

10 In which 1924 short did Fernand Léger create abstract, rhythmical patterns out of everyday sights?

11 Which American-born twins have produced such darkly mysterious pieces as *Street of Crocodiles* and *The Sleepwalkers of Daylight*?

12 What transport would you have to take to find the Blue Meanies, the Nowhere Man and the Sea of Time?

★ Who drew the first Mickey Mouse cartoon, *Plane Crazy*, as well as working on the effects for Hitchcock's *The Birds*?

TB Where could you find bumper cars bumping, cooked chickens dancing, and a room full of swirling furniture?

[14]

THE GREAT WAR

(S) Which army's point of view does *All Quiet on the Western Front* show?

1   Who singlehandedly captured 132 German soldiers during the Meuse-Argonne offensive?

2   And who won his first Oscar portraying him?

3   What two kinds of ship of the desert does *Lawrence of Arabia* see?

4   Which director, better known for his horror outings, directed *Journey's End* in 1930?

5   In *Civilisation*, who appears in a vision over the battlefields and inspires peace?

6   What kind of war is it when a cricket scoreboard is recording the tally of deaths?

7   When Archy (Mark Lee) and Frank (Mel Gibson) practise their war games under the pyramids, where are they practising for?

8   What paths lead, via a hopeless assault on 'the Anthill', to three scapegoat executions?

9   In *La Grande Illusion*, Erich von Stroheim's Commandant is concerned that the War will mean an end to what?

10   In *All Quiet on the Western Front*, what is Paul Baumer (Lew Ayres) doing when he's shot?

11   Which theatre of the War garnered the first ever Best Picture Oscar?

12   What was the sequel to *All Quiet on the Western Front*?

★   Who played the inept, callous General Broulard in *Paths of Glory*?

TB   Name the General, played by Jack Hawkins in *Lawrence of Arabia*, who eventually took Jerusalem from the Turks.

[15]
SCHINDLER'S LIST

(5) 'By this evening,' says Amon Goeth, 'those six centuries will be a rumour. They never happened.' What six centuries?

1 From whose novel is *Schindler's List* adapted?

2 As Oskar Schindler (Liam Neeson) tells Itzhak Stern (Ben Kingsley), he's not good at production work itself, but ... what?

3 Who played Amon Goeth?

4 What is the name of the Foundation Spielberg set up after making the film to catalogue as many accounts of Holocaust survivors as possible?

5 Schindler tells Stern that he will be very unhappy if his factory ever produces a shell that ... what?

6 When Schindler says, 'I want my people', what is Goeth's reply?

7 Goeth is the commandant of which labour camp?

8 'Whoever saves one life, saves ...' What?

9 'I pardon you', says Goeth, trying out the idea of mercy like a spoilt child with a new toy. Quickly bored, what does he do?

10 Who composed the soundtrack?

11 How long had it been since a black and white film won the Best Picture Oscar: 23, 33, 43 or 53 years?

12 Whose Oscar-winning film upset Spielberg so much that his wife had to restrain him from walking out of the cinema?

★ After the events shown in the film, where and how did Goeth die?

TB How many Oscars did *Schindler's List* win?

[16]
ITALIAN CINEMA

(S) Who gave Lamberto Maggiorani and Enzo Staiola a major problem?

1 Why was a bicycle so vital to Maggiorani?

2 What name was given to the gritty school of post-war Italian directors that included Roberto Rossellini, Vittorio de Sica and Luchino Visconti?

3 Who became obsessed with a beautiful boy in Visconti's *Death in Venice*?

4 What miracle helped the poor to fly away on broomsticks to a better world?

5 Who directed *La Dolce Vita*, *Eight and a Half* and *La Strada*?

6 Which Antonioni film told of a sailing trip to a remote island, where one of the party vanishes?

7 Visconti's *The Leopard* was based on whose account of life at the time of Garibaldi?

8 What connects Ingrid Bergman and 1945's *Open City*, about Roman resistance to the Nazis?

9 Who found Anita Ekberg bathing in a fountain in *La Dolce Vita*?

10 What exactly is the *Blow-Up* in Antonioni's 1966 film?

11 Which Roman studios were central to the growth of the Italian film industry in the fifties?

12 Which 1963 Fellini film was described by Pauline Kael as 'A deluxe glorification of creative crisis'?

★ The bitter post-war colonial struggles between France and Algeria were painstakingly documented in which Gillo Pontecorvo film of 1965?

TB What kind of paradise did Antonelli Attli, Enzo Cannavale, Ennio Morricone and Giuseppe Tornatore contribute to in 1989?

[17]
THE HOLLYWOOD MOGULS

(S) For which Methodist did 'Bombardier' Wells bang a gong?

1 According to a 1930 observer, 'There's nothing wrong with Hollywood that six first-class ... couldn't solve.' What?

2 Who was the second M in MGM?

3 Who headed Columbia for so long that he said 'Gower Street is paved with the bones of my executive producers'?

4 Al Jolson couldn't imagine what Jack Warner could do with an Oscar. Why?

5 Adolph Zukor was still on the roster of which studio when he died at the age of 103?

6 David Puttnam became production head at which studio in 1986, only to quit a year later in disgust?

7 Who supposedly said, 'Directors are always biting the hand that lays the golden egg'?

8 Who was production head at Universal at 21, ditto at MGM at 25, and dead at 37?

9 'Uncle Carl Laemmle has a very large faemmle.' The point being?

10 And why was Columbia once known as the Pine Tree Studio?

11 Darryl F Zanuck wanted to remake *Air Force* in what setting?

12 What film did David O. Selznick bring Hitchcock to America to make?

★ 'For God's sake, don't say yes until I finish talking!' Democracy whose style?

TB Was Louis B. Mayer born in Minsk, Omsk, Tomsk or Bulgaria?

[18]

THE ADVENT OF SOUND

(S) 'You ain't heard nothin' yet!' The film?

1   Only some parts of *The Jazz Singer* had synchronised sound. What was Hollywood's first '100% all-talkie'?

2   What was the 'Big Five Agreement', signed in 1927 by MGM, Universal, First National, Paramount and the Producers' Distributing Corporation?

3   Which studio was created to take advantage of the system which the 'Big Five' rejected, Photophone?

4   Who had marketed the Kinetophone, with synchronised sound, as early as 1895?

5   Why were the first sound camera booths called 'iceboxes'?

6   And why in the first days of sound did orchestras play live on set?

7   What was Hitchcock's first talkie?

8   Who directed *The Jazz Singer*?

9   What was a camera blimp?

10 For which silent film were turntables taken on the road to play records of 'machine gun fire' during the dogfight scenes?

11 Which actress complained, 'They made me sound as if I had been castrated'?

12 Which country came up with the Tri-Ergon system?

★   'Only the contrapuntal use of sound *vis-à-vis* the visual fragment of montage will open up new possibilities for the development and perfection of montage.' Whose snappy pronouncement on sound?

TB Who starred in the 1980 remake of *The Jazz Singer*?

[19]
ALFRED HITCHCOCK

(S) At which motel is it advisable not to take a shower?

1   In *Spellbound*, why did Gregory Peck have anxiety attacks at the sight of lines on a white background?

2   'Last night I dreamt I went to Manderley again.' Which film?

3   Who witnessed, or rather didn't witness, Raymond Burr murdering his wife in his apartment?

4   Which Hitchcock movie consists of a handful of extremely long takes?

5   Where were Robert Donat and Madeleine Carroll handcuffed together, and in which film?

6   Who was afraid of *The Birds*, but in real life went on to keep big cats?

7   Who helped design the dream sequence in *Spellbound*?

8   What had Hitch apparently used for blood in *Psycho*'s shower scene?

9   Who said that Hitchcock had 'given audiences more pleasure than is permissible for serious cinema'?

10 What proposition did Robert Walker make to Farley Granger in *Strangers on a Train*?

11 In which film did James Stewart save Kim Novak from drowning in San Francisco Bay?

12 Who did Joan Fontaine fear had murderous intent in *Suspicion*?

★   Whose character do we see shooting himself in Point Of View shot at the end of *Spellbound*?

TB After Hitch pronounced that 'Actors are cattle', who replied by driving some cattle onto the set?

[20]

SOVIET AND
RUSSIAN CINEMA

(5) Who said, 'Of all the arts, for us the cinema is the most important'?

1 Whose first feature was the war film *Ivan's Childhood*, in 1962?

2 Who had *Extraordinary Adventures … in the Land of the Bolsheviks*?

3 Who built bridges during the Civil War, and ever after compared film-making to bridge-building?

4 What artistic movement championed by Vsevolod Meyerhold saw a play or film as a machine, and its actors as biomechanical components?

5 In which month were the … *Ten Days that Shook the World*?

6 Which hero of a 1934 film demonstrates military strategy with potatoes?

7 Who directed *Mother*?

8 What non-naval character on *The Battleship Potemkin* stands for reactionary authority?

9 Who, as depicted by Tarkovsky in 1965, reacted to an unjust world by giving up speaking, painting and faith?

10 Who was the *Man with a Movie Camera*?

11 Who was the glasnost-liberated heroine of Vasily Pichul's 1988 film?

12 In *Swan Lake: The Zone* (1990), where does a fugitive from a prison camp hide out?

★ In 1930 the Soviet film industry was nationalised into what single company: Mirkino, Kinopravda, Soyuzkino, Kinosalyut or Stalinkino?

TB *Arsenal* and *Earth*. The director?

[21]

THE WESTERN

(S) Who were Brad Dexter, James Coburn, Charles Bronson, Horst Buckholz, Robert Vaughn, Steve McQueen and Yul Brynner?

1 'Do not forsake me, oh my darling …' Who was forsaken by all his townsfolk in *High Noon*?

2 Which tale of a homesteader family helped by a mysterious stranger, as always, tried to make Alan Ladd as tall as possible?

3 Who kept calling Richard Harris the Duck instead of the Duke? In which movie?

4 Who was Bob Hope when he sang *Buttons and Bows*?

5 In which films did the wonderfully dry Chief Dan George appear opposite Dustin Hoffman and Clint Eastwood?

6 'He was no bum, was he? But he never gave me any manure about art.' Which director was John Wayne talking about?

7 Which gravel-voiced tough guy actor was the unlikely winner of a Best Song Oscar in *Paint Your Wagon*?

8 Who directed the story of the Union Pacific railroad builders, though he is not best known for his Westerns?

9 It lasted just 10 minutes, but in 1903 it was the first Western. What?

10 Which two *Fistfuls* did Sergio Leone direct?

11 Who was *The Man from Laramie* and *The Man who Shot Liberty Valance*?

12 What film saw a horse get lynched along with its rider, and the world's most flatulent campfire meal?

★ Which tale of Clark Gable's and Spencer Tracy's oil-drilling fortunes had more ups and downs than a nodding derrick?

TB An Italian Spaghetti Western actor named himself Clint Southwood. True or false?

[22]

THE FILM IMAGE

(S) Which Steven Spielberg film has deliberately desaturated colour?

1   Who had Bedouin tents distributed just so around Wadi Rumm to create the perfect establishing shot?

2   What do f-stops control?

3   What was the 'triptych' format which Abel Gance experimented with in *Napoleon*?

4   In which film do rival Japanese clans fight a sea battle against a stylised red and yellow sky?

5   Robbers stride into an Edinburgh John Menzies, as seen reflected upside-down in its façade. The film?

6   What is an iris-out?

7   Who was a second-unit cameraman on *Lawrence of Arabia*, before showing what he could do as director with *Walkabout* and *Don't Look Now*?

8   Who can we thank for the photography of *The Grapes of Wrath* and *Citizen Kane*?

9   What name is given to the primary and strongest light in a shot?

10 Where do semi-abstracted violin bows dance to Bach's *Toccata and Fugue*?

11 When *Butch Cassidy and the Sundance Kid* discard their bicycle, why does its spinning wheel become sepia-tinted?

12 An eye blinks and blinks, and between each blink the screen turns a different colour, until finally normality returns. The film?

★   Is Renoir's *La Régle du Jeu* notable for extreme depth of field photography, for highly-compressed perspective through use of long lenses, or for *film noir* chiaroscuro?

TB Name the film where a city's burning gas plumes are reflected in a human eye.

[23]

MARTIN SCORSESE

(S) Is Travis Bickle a Taxi Driver, a Goodfella, a King of Comedy or a Raging Bull?

1 The camera follows Ray Liotta and Lorraine Bracco across the street, down the stairs, through corridors and kitchens into a club. In a single shot. The film?

2 Who really played himself as the veteran funnyman whom crazed Robert De Niro idolises in *The King of Comedy*?

3 Griffin Dunne. Teri Garr. A quirky odyssey through the New York night. The title?

4 What movie is based on the life of boxer Jake La Motta?

5 What eventually happened to La Motta, physically and professionally?

6 Who are Robbie Robertson, Levon Helm, Garth Hudson, Richard Manuel and Rick Danko, and what was Scorsese's document of their farewell concert?

7 Name the electrifying actor who played De Niro's brother in *Raging Bull* and his partner in crime in *Goodfellas*

8 Which role became rather more graphic in the thirty years between Robert Mitchum's and Robert De Niro's performances?

9 Why were Liotta, de Niro and Pesci in particular trouble for killing Frank Vincent?

10 Which controversial interpretation of the Gospel accounts caused as much of a scene as *Life of Brian*, although its intentions were more serious?

11 Which period piece is to date the only appearance Daniel Day-Lewis has made for Scorsese?

12 If you're looking for Alice, what do Ellen Burstyn and Alfred Lutter know?

★ What use did Travis make of a sliding rail?

TB Which usual Scorsese suspects turned up in reprises of past roles in *Casino*?

[24]
DREAMS AND FANTASIES

(**S**) Who came to get yer if you had *A Nightmare on Elm Street*?

1 Where should you beware of men who are hairy on the inside?

2 Who said, 'We are the music makers, and we are the dreamers of dreams'?

3 Which Frank L. Baum fable was *Zardoz* a corruption of?

4 Whose version of *Alice*, a world of skeleton beasts and dark deeds through the drawer of a table, was truer to the dark spirit of the book than the anodyne Disney version?

5 A woman having her eyeball slit open is the attention-seeking start of which surrealist classic?

6 Which talent links *The Thief of Bagdad*, *A Canterbury Tale* and *Peeping Tom*?

7 What does the title of Ingmar Bergman's *The Seventh Seal* refer to?

8 Who were the comic duo who played rivals in golf and love, even beyond the grave, in *Dead of Night*?

9 Why were a boy and girl fleeing from a preacher with LOVE and HATE tattooed on his knuckles? The movie?

10 What proportion of the testimonies in Kurosawa's *Rashomon* are told by ghosts?

11 Of what fable did Jean Cocteau say,
'It is a drama of the visible and the invisible ... I interwove many myths. Death condemns herself in order to help the man she is duty bound to destroy'?

12 Tim the Enchanter. The Knights who say 'Ni'. 'Run away, run away' . . . Stop it – what quest is getting silly?

★ Which Brothers Quay animation found a man wandering a decayed world of wind-up monkeys, screws with a life of their own, grimy windows and malignant dolls with empty heads?

TB What was the Oogie Boogie Man, the real nightmare in *The Nightmare Before Christmas*, made of?

[25]

TITANIC

(5) How did Jack Dawson come by his ticket for the *Titanic*?

1 'It's been 84 years, and I can still smell the fresh paint. The china had never been used. The sheets had never been slept in. *Titanic* was called the ship of dreams and it was, it really was.' The speaker?

2 Who is Rose Bukater engaged to?

3 Which shipping line did the *Titanic* belong to: the White Star Line, the Blue Star Line, Cunard or P&O?

4 What was *Titanic*'s estimated budget?

5 'You have a gift, Jack. You see people. You do.' Jack's reply?

6 What's unusual about Kate Winslet's and Gloria Stuart's Oscar nominations (for Best Actress and Best Supporting Actress respectively)?

7 Which two studios shared the burden of *Titanic*'s budget?

8 How large was the reconstructed *Titanic* in relation to the original?

9 Which rescue ship was the first to arrive on the scene?

10 Rose Bukater comes from one of the best families in: New York, Boston, Pittsburgh or Philadelphia?

11 What happened when Jack's friend Tommy Ryan tried to get into one of the lifeboats?

12 Did the *Titanic* set sail from Liverpool, Southampton, Dublin or New York?

★ What was Jack's cabin number?

TB Who was the richest passenger on the *Titanic*?

[26]

SPECIAL EFFECTS

(5) Why is the colour of the screen used for superimposing shots usually blue?

1 How did the father of special effects, Georges Méliès, achieve the trick of *The Man with the Rubber Head*?

2 What name is given to the technique of moving a model slightly, exposing a frame, and repeating the process, as *King Kong*, the first great monster movie, exemplified?

3 In which film did Bob Hoskins have to do most of his acting to an empty space, into which characters were later animated?

4 What is a matte painting?

5 For which film, of a boy who helps a king regain his crown from a usurper, did Lawrence Butler produce magical early Technicolor effects?

6 Who provided the slightly creaky miniature monster effects for *Jason and the Argonauts* and *Sinbad and the Eye of the Tiger*?

7 In sound effects, what are 'whoop-whoops'?

8 Which early horror film used every trick in the book, including cutting out individual frames to make the villain creepily jerky, reversed action, and double exposures, to unnerve the viewer?

9 For which film was a giant Ferris-Wheel-like set built, to give the impression of a spacecraft bridge with centrifugal gravity?

10 What name is given to animating real people frame by frame, as if they were animated models?

11 Which film depicted a tiny cameraman with his tripod, standing on top of a camera?

12 Which wildlife reserve comprised creatures who only existed inside Silicon Graphics workstations?

★ How can you alter the frame-per-second speed to give a miniature model a feeling of size and weight?

TB The latest T1000 model is made of liquid metal, well-suited to the computer morphing techniques of the early nineties. Which film?

[27]

AKIRA KUROSAWA

(S) Under what name was *Seven Samurai* released in America?

1 Which of Kurosawa's films did George Lucas acknowledge as inspiration for the plot of *Star Wars*?

2 How did Kurosawa foreshorten near and far objects to create a flattened effect?

3 What two crimes did a woodcutter witness in *Rashomon*?

4 What connection does *Throne of Blood* have with Scotland?

5 When Kurosawa said that he would prefer to be fêted for contemporary rather than period dramas, what celebrated Italian film did he hold up as an example?

6 After Kurosawa had fallen out of favour with the Japanese film industry, which western fans helped finance *Kagemusha* and *Ran*?

7 Which of *Rashomon*'s four witnesses, woodcutter, lady, bandit or ghost of the lord, gives the true account of the incident?

8 Who (inevitably) played the bandit?

9 Which film shows an X-ray of an elderly clerk's cancerous tumour?

10 What effect, used by Kurosawa to heighten violent actions, has been copied by Peckinpah and others to the point of cliché?

11 Who had arrows shot at him in *The Castle of the Spider's Web*, because Kurosawa felt that the original fakes looked bogus?

12 Is Kurosawa usually regarded as Japan's most 'western' director, as an artist mainly influenced by Chinese tradition, or as the best exponent of traditional Japanese film style?

★ Who played the leader of the *Seven Samurai* (Yul Brynner to Mifune's Horst Buckholz)?

TB How were King Lear and his three daughters changed for *Ran*?

[28]
STAR WARS

(S) *Star Wars* is set in the distant future, in a galaxy far, far away. True or false?

1 As he grew up on Tatooine, how many sunsets could Luke watch every night?

2 Why did Harrison Ford happen to be at George Lucas's studios, so that he got roped into the *Star Wars* casting sessions?

3 Who was Governor of the Imperial outland regions?

4 What throats did Producer Gary Kurtz have to slit with a razor blade, and why?

5 In what (unseasonally waterlogged) country were the Tatooine exteriors filmed?

6 Who are Tatooine's rag and bone men?

7 What warrior caste had been the guardians of the Old Republic?

8 What had been George Lucas's first feature film, an altogether bleaker view of the universe?

9 Who spent a day standing naked while being covered with vaseline and wet plaster, and why?

10 'What a piece of junk ...' What was Luke talking about?

11 What was done to Carrie Fisher's bust for the filming?

12 Who said, 'Acting in this movie, I felt like a raisin in a giant fruit salad. And I didn't even know who the coconuts or the cantaloupes were'?

★ Which classic movie character was the inspiration for an originally female C3PO?

TB Why apparently was R2-D2 so named?

[29]

CINEMA IN
WORLD WAR II

(S) What was the objective in 1945 for Errol Flynn and Raoul Walsh?

1 For which documentary did John Huston use the voices of dead soldiers, as recorded before battle, over shots of their dead bodies?

2 What happened to this footage?

3 Was Cary Grant trying to get to *Destination Tokyo* by parachute drop, by ship, by submarine or in the guise of a diplomat?

4 What anti-Semitic German film of 1940 depicted an evil eighteenth century Jewish moneylender?

5 Who played Rommel in *Five Graves to Cairo*?

6 Which Noel Coward film dramatised the exploits of Lord Mountbatten and *HMS Kelly*, sunk during the Battle of Crete?

7 What series of documentaries included *Prelude to War*, *Divide and Conquer* and *War Comes to America*?

8 Whose pet project was *Kolberg*, a lavish German equivalent of *Gone with the Wind*?

9 Why did the interior of Canterbury Cathedral have to be reconstructed in Denham Studios for *A Canterbury Tale*?

10 During the making of which documentary was John Ford wounded by enemy fire?

11 Was *Western Approaches* a tribute to the Royal Navy, the Merchant Navy, or the citizens of America?

12 What was Britain's *Desert Victory*?

★ Which Humphrey Jennings film was scripted by E.M. Forster, and attempted to explain the experiences of the War to the post-war generation?

TB In which country did weekly cinema attendances rise from 19 million in 1939 to 30 million in 1945?

[30]

D.W. GRIFFITH

(S) The publicity read, 'The dawn of a new art!' The film?

1 Who said that Griffith 'was the first to photograph thought'?

2 Was Griffith's father 'Roaring Jake', a Confederate Civil War hero, Thomas Edison, an assumer of credit for other people's ideas, or William Wilberforce, an anti-slavery campaigner?

3 Who played the Eternal Mother in *Intolerance*?

4 Which organisation is portrayed as rescuing heroes in *Birth of a Nation*?

5 Name either of the directors with whom Griffith formed the Triangle Corporation in 1915

6 In 1918, Griffith tactfully said, 'Viewed as drama, [it] is somewhat disappointing.' What?

7 *Intolerance* was a hefty fourteen reels in length. Roughly how long is that?

8 Which of the following is not a Griffith short of 1908: *Romance of a Jewess*, *Zulu's Heart*, *Love the Stranger in Thy Midst* or *Ingomar the Barbarian*?

9 Under what title did *Birth of a Nation* premiere in Los Angeles?

10 Woodrow Wilson described *Birth of a Nation* as 'like writing history with …' What?

11 Did *Intolerance*'s massacre of 1572 happen on Whitsun, St Swithin's Day, St Bartholomew's Day or Mothering Sunday?

12 Griffith's first sound picture was an epic biography of whom?

★ Name either of the families caught up on opposing sides in *Birth of a Nation*.

TB Who, on receiving his D. W. Griffith Award shortly before his death, compared Griffith to Icarus?

[31]
WORLD CLASSICS

(5) Who did David Lean introduce to the world after a career in Egyptian films?

1 Which beautiful Chinese actress starred in *Ju Dou*, *Raise the Red Lantern* and *Farewell My Concubine*?

2 Who directed *Persona*, about a psychiatric nurse who becomes increasingly intertwined with her patient?

3 Which country gave us *Aan*, *The World of Apu* and *The Chess Players*?

4 Name the Danish director of classics *The Passion of Joan of Arc* and *Vampyr*.

5 When *Hill 24 Does Not Answer*, which beleaguered nation is concerned?

6 Which luminous Tarkovsky work centred on Russia's finest icon painter?

7 Does the bleak, haunting *Alpine Fire* come from Germany, Austria, Switzerland or France?

8 Name the actor who, in *Yojimbo*, provided the blueprint for Clint Eastwood's Man with No Name.

9 Who was the Argentinean director of *The Fall* and *The House of the Angel*?

10 *Women on the Verge of a Nervous Breakdown. High Heels. Tie Me Up! Tie Me Down!* The Spanish king of kitsch?

11 How does the hero of *The Vanishing* end up?

12 Where can you see a shadow warrior and colour-coordinated armies?

★ What kind of workplace provides the striking colour schemes of *Ju Dou*?

TB Which country produces more feature films than Hollywood?

[32]

TIM BURTON

(S) Which of the following was directed by Tim Burton: *Superman*, *Batman* or *The Man Who Shot Liberty Valance*?

1 At which studio did Burton work as an animator, before deciding that their output was too conventional for his taste?

2 His first significant solo animation was a tribute to which grand old man of horror?

3 'Bug … breakfast drink …'What's Winona Ryder trying to say?

4 Who went from *Catch-22* to playing the myopic patriarch of *Edward Scissorhands*?

5 The composer of *The Simpsons'* theme tune is also Burton's regular musical collaborator. Who is he?

6 Which film gave us the irony of one of Hollywood's most gifted directors crafting a loving tribute to one of its worst?

7 Why might a beehive hairdo give grounds for suspicion in *Mars Attacks*?

8 In which town might you find a yowling cat siren, a coffin that's also a double-bass, and a girl who is forever having to sew her limbs back on?

9 Who do Lock, Shock and Barrel kidnap, mistakenly believing him to be Sandy Claws?

10 Who had little difficulty convincingly portraying the ill-starred lovers of *Edward Scissorhands*?

11 Who had a *Big Adventure*?

12 Which of the following skills doesn't Edward Scissorhands exhibit: ice sculpture, topiary, hairdressing, sheep-shearing or dog-clipping?

★ Is the animation style in *A Nightmare Before Christmas* called substitution animation, cell animation, computer-generated animation or armature puppet animation?

TB Is *Frankenweenie* a dog, a hot dog, a frog or a bog monster?

[33]
ALEC GUINNESS

(S) Who called *Oliver Twist* 'Owiver'?

1   What was built to the whistling of *Colonel Bogie*?

2   Where was the spiral staircase that Guinness and Stanley Holloway ran down, laughing deliriously, in *The Lavender Hill Mob*?

3   Which of Guinness's characters yearned to see Damascus?

4   What did Damascus have while London was only a village?

5   Was George Smiley a *Tinker*, a *Tailor*, a *Soldier*, or what?

6   In which film did Guinness play eight family members?

7   And what happened to his photographic enthusiast?

8   Which character was conceived as a cross between Gandalf, a Mexican sorcerer and a samurai?

9   In *Tunes of Glory*, Guinness's hard-drinking old lag and John Mills's strait-laced newcomer crossed swords over the running of what organisation?

10   What was so pleasant about *The Captain's Paradise*?

11   In *Kind Hearts and Coronets*, what dreadful mistake did Dennis Price make when he was reprieved from the gallows?

12   'Why don't you give this line to the little green thing?' What was 'the little green thing'?

★   Who helped Pip help Magwitch escape from the authorities?

TB   How did the last of *The Ladykillers* die?

[34]
DARK FUTURES

(S) Why was *The Terminator* trying to kill Sarah Connor?

1 Who lived in a world of gleaming whites, shaven heads, robot policemen, and a society numbed into subservience by drugs?

2 What was important about the number thirty in *Logan's Run*?

3 What ship's crew had to convince a philosophical bomb that it didn't exist to prevent it going off?

4 Art director Anton Furst's greatest achievement was the future-gothic design of which city?

5 In what movie were the crew of a mining ship violated not only by a parasitic monster, but by employers willing to sacrifice them for military knowledge?

6 Which Terry Gilliam feature was never properly released because he refused to sweeten its bleak ending?

7 Who or what skinned Jim Hopper and his troops in a South American jungle?

8 What was the Army of the *Twelve Monkeys*: (a) slang for a government genetic warfare establishment, (b) a religious order of mutants, or (c) an animal liberation group?

9 Whose vision of a future Los Angeles was a rain-soaked, blue-washed world of ziggurats, Japanese slang, and people and animals made to order?

10 'Get away from her, you *bitch!*' In *Aliens*, how was Ripley talking from a position of strength?

11 Who kept law and order in a dystopian Detroit ruled by corporate interest, where you could buy games like *Nuke Em* and cars like the 6000 SUX?

12 Who went to pieces in a liquid nitrogen spill in *Terminator 2: Judgement Day*?

★ Who began to turn into metal after a Japanese road accident?

TB Why for a long time were you unlikely to have seen a horrorshow film about droogs?

[35]

THE MUSICAL

5 *West Side Story* is based on which play?

1 *On the Town*. Which town?

2 Where are we taught to do the Timewarp?

3 The birth pangs of what development in Hollywood were spoofed in *Singing in the Rain*?

4 Who played Porgy in Otto Preminger's *Porgy and Bess*?

5 Raindrops on roses, soft woollen mittens, brown paper packages tied up with string ... These are a few of what?

6 Who wrote *Count Your Blessings*, and lived to be 101?

7 *No Strings (I'm Fancy Free)*, *Isn't This a Lovely Day (To Be Caught in the Rain?)*, *Cheek to Cheek*. Who and who in what?

8 'Consider yourself at home! Consider yourself part of the family!' What family is this?

9 Name the gangs and their ethnic make-ups in *West Side Story*.

10 Why do Gene Kelly, Frank Sinatra and Jules Munshin have only 24 hours to spend in New York?

11 If it is *Oh, What a Beautiful Morning!*, what part of America are you in?

12 *The Philadelphia Story* was remade as a musical under what title?

★ Name a musical based on Plautus.

TB What kind of diggers dug between 1933 and 1937?

[36]
AUSTRALIAN CINEMA

(S) When Holly Hunter arrived in New Zealand to marry a landowner, what did she have to leave on the beach?

1 This ethereal tale, one of the most successfully mystical of feature films, of three turn of the century schoolgirls who vanish at the landmark of the title, marked the beginning of a healthy period for Australian cinema. What is it?

2 Who fought Japanese troops, Turkish troops and road warriors before discovering the joys of painting your face blue?

3 What was the tragic story of *The Chant of Jimmie Blacksmith*?

4 During a *Long Weekend* of persecution by homicidal wildlife, how are the couple killed?

5 What message was Mel Gibson not quite sprinter enough to deliver at *Gallipoli*?

6 Before *Miami Vice*, where did we see Don Johnson accompanied by a telepathic dog in an apocalyptic future with a memorable ending?

7 Was *Breaker Morant* the tale (a) of the bittersweet ups and downs of an Aussie Rules football club, (b) of Boer War officers court-martialled for killing prisoners, or (c) of a backward young labourer who falls for an older American woman?

8 Who moved from the otherworldliness of *Picnic at Hanging Rock* to Hollywood, where the story of an otherworldly US community garnered him an Oscar nomination?

9 Which pop star turned up in the druggy squat scene film, *Dogs in Space*?

10 Before finding fame and husband in Hollywood, who starred with Denholm Elliott in the TV drama of a woman arrested in Thailand for drug trafficking?

11 Which director made the dingo baby drama, *A Cry in the Dark*, for Hollywood?

12 What was the Stinson of *The Riddle of the Stinson*?

★ Long before the Australian film renaissance of the seventies, who was turning out actioners like *The Rats of Tobruk, Forty Thousand Horsemen* and *In the Wake of the Bounty*?

TB Who handcuffed a villain's ankle to the bumper of a car rigged to explode, and gave him a hacksaw to cut his foot off?

[37]

POWELL
AND PRESSBURGER

(5) 'One is so starved of Technicolor up there!' Where?

1   Who menaced young ladies in *A Canterbury Tale*?

2   And how did *Peeping Tom* murder his victims?

3   What nationality was Emeric Pressburger?

4   When Colonel Blimp was captured in wargames because the other side had cheated, what point was being made?

5   How does Abu trick the great genie back into his bottle in *The Thief of Baghdad*?

6   'The ballet is my career, not the cinema, Mr Powell.' The star of *The Red Shoes*?

7   What is *Black Narcissus*?

8   And in *Black Narcissus*, who plays the native girl who entrances Sabu?

9   Who has doubts about her intended marriage while a storm keeps her from getting to the Hebrides?

10 What did Powell and Pressburger call themselves?

11 Who 'seeks the eternal woman, and is beset by eternal evil'?

12 How did Ralph Richardson sacrifice his life to thwart the Nazis in *The Silver Fleet*?

★   Name any one of the other five people given directing credits with Powell on *The Thief of Baghdad*.

TB Which German ship was run to ground in *The Battle of the River Plate*?

[38]
TRAINSPOTTING

(S) Where is *Trainspotting* set: Edinburgh, Glasgow, Dundee or Tunbridge Wells?

1 Begbie doesn't do drugs. What *does* he do?

2 Renton's mother is, in her own socially acceptable way, an addict, addicted to ...?

3 Which movie star and long-time non-resident Scot is Sick Boy obsessed with?

4 No longer constipated, Renton fantasises about pristine conveniences and silken paper. (Precisely) what does he get instead?

5 What does Iggy Pop have at the start of the film?

6 And what does Diane think Iggy's name is?

7 The night with Diane's the best Renton's felt since ...?

8 What surprise does Diane spring on Renton the morning after?

9 How does Tommy die?

10 When going cold turkey, what does Renton hallucinate on his bedroom ceiling?

11 What's the happy ending for Renton?

12 And the happy ending for Spud?

★ In which TV series does Robert Carlyle stab Christopher Ecclestone to death?

TB What is the only colour in *Trainspotting*'s poster ad campaign?

[39]
ROCK 'N' ROLL

(S) Who had to rescue Pepperland from the Blue Meanies?

1 Levon Helm, who played Sissy Spacek's father in *Coal Miner's Daughter*, is better known as the drummer with which band?

2 Who was *The Man who Fell to Earth*?

3 Which siblings were told by the proprietor of a redneck bar that both types of music were played there: country and western?

4 *Blue Hawaii, Girls! Girls! Girls!, Fun in Acapulco*. Vehicles for whom?

5 Which heavy metal band lost a member because he choked on someone else's vomit?

6 Who goes down on bended knee before his dream guitar, and whispers 'Excalibur!'?

7 What do the Beatles keep praising Wilfred Brambell for in *A Hard Day's Night*?

8 Who played the Pinball Wizard, with mile-high platform boots, in *Tommy*?

9 What went wrong with Spinal Tap's Stonehenge stage set?

10 In which city was Elvis due to compete in a Grand Prix against Count Elmo Mancini?

11 Who profiled Bob Dylan in *Don't Look Back*?

12 Who played Buddy Holly in a 1978 biopic?

★ Which DJ played himself in *American Graffiti*?

TB 'Why don't you come up to the lab, and see what I've got on the slab?' Tim Curry's Transylvanian transsexual mad scientist?

[40]
RIDLEY SCOTT

(S) If it is Los Angeles, in November 2019, then what is Harrison Ford?

1 Which 1992 film demonstrated how to make sail, hawsers and high seas look wonderfully cinematic?

2 What famous slogan was used to advertise *Alien*?

3 Before Hollywood, did Scott create a stir with a television ad for (a) Long Life milk, (b) Rennie indigestion tablets, or (c) Hovis bread?

4 What was the real purpose of the transmission the *Nostromo* thought was a distress signal?

5 Where did the great Tim Curry play a horned demon?

6 What fail-safe was built into replicants, in case they became too human?

7 Who went on a crime spree across the southern USA after killing a would-be rapist?

8 And who was the cop on their trail?

9 'I've seen things you wouldn't believe. Attack ships on fire off the shoulder of Orion ...' Who played replicant Roy Batty, in a role that promised more than his subsequent career has delivered?

10 What two roles has Sigourney Weaver played for Scott?

11 What happened when John Hurt had a fit of indigestion?

12 And what colour was Ian Holm's blood?

★ What was Eldin Tyrrell's first inkling that somebody smarter was in the lift with J. F. Sebastian?

TB Who were Keith Carradine and Harvey Keitel?

[41]

EWAN MCGREGOR

⑤ Is McGregor's character in *Trainspotting* called Arthur Dent, Mark Renton or Mark Rylance?

1 Robert De Niro is to Marlon Brando as McGregor is to Alec Guinness. How?

2 'Even Master Yoda doesn't have a midi-chlorian count that high!' What's Obi-Wan talking about?

3 In which Dennis Potter TV series did McGregor spend most of his time grinning while heated musical fantasies erupted around him?

4 If McGregor has to put up with having his legs smashed, and a paranoid Christopher Ecclestone spying on him from the ceiling, then what's Keith Allen been buried in?

5 Why is Ecclestone furious with McGregor and Kerry Fox for buying a camcorder?

6 What kind of people are Holly Hunter and Delroy Lindo in *A Life Less Ordinary*, and what is their task?

7 Who directed *The Pillow Book*?

8 Name the dealer and the bank whose downfall are charted in *Rogue Trader*.

9 What is Qui-Gon Jinn's dying request to Obi-Wan?

10 Is *Velvet Goldmine* about late sixties psychedelia, glam rock, punk or new romanticism?

11 Who directed McGregor in *Shallow Grave* and *Trainspotting*?

12 In *A Life Less Ordinary*, why is Stanley Tucci doubly unsuited to treating McGregor's wound?

★ In *The Pillow Book*, McGregor and Vivian Wu write on each other. In which Japanese classic are prayers written on a young monk to protect him from ghosts?

TB 'Aye, for all the good they've done me, I might as well have stuck 'em up my arse!' What?

[42]

FILM AND TELEVISION

(5) Who's the only adult in Seahaven who doesn't know about *The Truman Show*?

1 Why, according to Ernie Kovacs, is television a medium?

2 Who filled Jack Lemmon's and Walter Matthau's shoes in *The Odd Couple*'s TV spin-off?

3 Why is a film's running time slightly shorter on TV or video?

4 Which TV series did George Clooney prudently hang on to despite being a big screen Batman?

5 Why did some big-name American screenwriters come and write for British television in the 1950s?

6 Which surgeon connects Donald Sutherland and Alan Alda?

7 Who played a murderer spied on by a man in a wheelchair, and a wheelchair-bound cop?

8 Name any three actors who have played *The Saint*, on big screen or small.

9 Who directed *Quiz Show*, based on the rigging of a 1950s TV programme?

10 Who gets a hallucinatory health warning from Dale Winton on the box in *Trainspotting*?

11 Who drove a Fiat Torino on TV, and made Arnold Schwarzenegger take a dangerous ride in a life-or-death gameshow?

12 Which character has been played by Burgess Meredith and Danny DeVito?

★ Who said, 'It used to be that films were the lowest form of art. Now we have something to look down on'?

TB Who's sucked through the TV screen in *Poltergeist*?

[43]
MARLON BRANDO

(S) 'I coulda had class. I coulda been a contender.' The union drama?

1   At which dramatic workshop did Lee Strasberg's tutelage help Brando develop his acting technique?

2   What injury had Brando's GI received in *The Men*?

3   Maria Schneider and a lump of butter. The film?

4   Why was Brando seen largely in static, low-lit shots in *Apocalypse Now*, revealing little but his head?

5   How did he appear in *The Teahouse of the August Moon*?

6   Who was Blanch to Brando's Stanley Kowalski in *A Streetcar Named Desire*?

7   In *Guys and Dolls*, who was the great singer who acted to Brando's great actor who sang?

8   What was Brando rebelling against in *The Wild One*?

9   What piece of whistleblowing was Elia Kazan accused of trying to justify in directing *On the Waterfront*?

10 Who played Brutus to Brando's Mark Antony in *Julius Caesar*?

11 Name Brando's renegade Colonel in *Apocalypse Now*, and the character he is based on.

12 For which apartheid drama was Brando tempted out of retirement in 1989?

★   What was Kurtz's dream and nightmare?

TB Why did Brando decline to accept his Oscar for *The Godfather*?

[44]
THE SILENT COMICS

⑤ Of whom did W. C. Fields say, 'The son of a bitch is a ballet dancer!'?

1 Which vaudeville impresario counted Charlie Chaplin and Stan Laurel among his alumni?

2 Who was known as Stoneface?

3 And what was *The General*?

4 What was Mack Sennett talking about when he said, 'Non-anticipation on the part of the recipient of the pastry is the chief ingredient of the recipe'?

5 Whose Hollywood career was crippled in 1921 by a sensational murder trial?

6 How long is a two-reeler?

7 Who experimented with screen personae such as Willie Work and Lonesome Luke, before settling on his boater and spectacles?

8 Which film saw Lloyd scaling a skyscraper to impress his girlfriend?

9 If you wanted proper policing, who didn't you call?

10 Who at the age of 100 was able to look back at the days when he produced Harold Lloyd and Laurel and Hardy?

11 Who perfected the 'slow-burn' as long-suffering stooge to many stars?

12 Which battle was the greatest custard-pie fight of them all?

★ Which French slapsticker took a bath and taught the tango, and probably influenced Chaplin's screen act?

TB What was most unusual about Chaplin's *Modern Times*, made in 1936?

[45]
EUROPEAN CINEMA

(5) Where do vegetarian terrorists wage war against a cannibal butcher?

1 In which political drama is Yves Montand assassinated by being clubbed in the head?

2 What does *Heimat* mean?

3 What were the nationalities of Irene Jacob's characters in *The Double Life of Veronique*?

4 Who had to assassinate a target in her underwear from a Venice bathroom?

5 What is the strangest quality of the planet Solaris in Tarkovsky's 1972 film?

6 In *Europa, Europa*, what is unusual about Josef Peters, a translator for a German Army unit on the eastern front?

7 Which country has given us *My Life as a Dog*, *Dog Days* and *Hour of the Wolf*?

8 Who played Octave in Jean Renoir's *La Régle du Jeu*?

9 What is the homeland of István Szabó, Bela Lugosi and Mischa Auer?

10 Which red-haired actress regularly stars for Pedro Almodóvar?

11 Name the Elem Klimov film which saw the horrors of the Byelorussian front through a boy soldier's eyes?

12 Name the middle film of Andrzej Wajda's trilogy, bookended by *A Generation* and *Ashes and Diamonds*.

★ What is the importance of the 'kanaly' of *Kanal*?

TB What is the hero's final fate in George Sluizer's *The Vanishing*?

[46]
JOHN FORD

(S) 'But we keep a-comin'. We're the people that live. Can't lick us. We'll go on forever, Pa, because we're the people.' Which film?

1   Which patrol included Boris Karloff, Reginald Denny and Victor McLaglen?

2   Mose Harper wants nothing more for services rendered than to while away his days in a rocking-chair. In which film?

3   Who busted a man's head with a shovel for sticking a knife in him, and was let out after four years?

4   What natural disaster forced thousands like the Joads to leave their farmsteads and head for work in California?

5   Which regular Ford star could match the director with a list of over 125 movies?

6   Against which organisation was The Informer informing?

7   From which western of a misconstrued hero comes the line, 'When truth becomes legend, print the legend'?

8   For which kind of camerawork was Ford famous: (a) multi-layered, ironic montage sequences, (b) plain, static shots, sympathetic to character, or (c) dreamlike processions of half-glimpsed visions?

9   In which film did John Wayne play the Ringo Kid, a wanted man who eventually redeems himself?

10 Who played Young Mr Lincoln?

11 Who were The Searchers, and who exactly were they looking for?

12 Why respectively were Doc Boone and Dallas considered undesirable by the townsfolk of Tonto?

★   In which film does retiring Cavalry Captain Nathan Brittles stand beside his still horse, while we hear the hoofbeats of the patrol he would still like to be riding with?

TB Where was Henry Fonda Wyatt Earp, setting Tombstone to rights and sorting out the Clantons in a forerunner to Gunfight at the OK Corral?

[47]
JAMES BOND

(S) Who is Goldfinger's heavy with the razor-rimmed bowler, played by wrestler Harold Sakata?

1 What favourite possession was Bond asked to surrender in *Dr No*?

2 Of what crime organisation is Ernst Stavro Blofeld the head?

3 What is Bond's military rank?

4 Which Albanian monarch did Ian Fleming, himself a Naval intelligence officer, help to escape the Nazis?

5 Who wrote *The Times* obituary for Fleming's father, MP Valentine Fleming?

6 In *Thunderball*, how did the world's leaders signal their acceptance of Blofeld's demands?

7 Who is Bond's CIA counterpart?

8 How does Bond turn the tables on Robert Shaw's Red Grant on the Orient Express?

9 What was the specialism of Jane Seymour's Solitaire in *You Only Live Twice*: code-breaking, fortune-telling, linguistics or taekwondo?

10 What does SPECTRE stand for?

11 Who wrote the title song for *Goldeneye*?

12 Whose power of voodoo in *You Only Live Twice* didn't save him from the *Alien*?

★ Who was the first James Bond ever to appear on screen?

TB What was odd about Scaramanga's chest?

[48]

JAPANESE CINEMA

(S) Which Akira Kurosawa film, itself influenced by Hollywood westerns, was the inspiration for *The Magnificent Seven*?

1 Which Kurosawa film related four eye-witness accounts of a murder, one of them told by a ghost?

2 Who or what is Noh?

3 What was the main theme of Yosujiro Ozu's *Tokyo Story*?

4 Who used very long takes, deep focus and complex camera movements in such films as *Naniwa Elegy*, *Sisters of Gion* and *The 47 Ronin*?

5 Which movie inspired *A Fistful of Dollars*?

6 What generic name is given to the stylish, often 18-rated, Japanese animations now popular worldwide?

7 Where did a clerk learn that he was terminally ill, and put the time left to good use?

8 Which ubiquitous actor provided a fierce presence in *Seven Samurai*, *Rashomon*, *Yojimbo*, and even *Hell in the Pacific* (with Lee Marvin)?

9 What was Kurosawa's version of *Lear*?

10 What is notable about the eyes of Western cartoon characters drawn in Japanese animation houses?

11 Who directed *Fires on the Plain*, about a soldier who goes mad in the Philippines and becomes a cannibal?

12 Which Japanese/French production detailed the romance between a French actress and a Japanese architect?

★ Which ghostly Mizoguchi film was taken from a collection of stories called *Tales of a Pale and Mysterious Moon after the Rain*?

TB Who or what was Kurosawa's *Kagemusha*?

[49]
CARY GRANT

(5) Where was Grant terrorised by a crop-duster plane?

1 'You remind me of a man ...'
'What man?'
'The man with the power ...'
'What power?'
'The power of hoodoo ...'
'Hoodoo?'
'You do'
'I do what?'
'Remind me of a man '
Who was the bobbysoxer Grant was teasing?

2 What kind of *Notorious* politics did Grant's contact Ingrid Bergman marry into?

3 'You're a better man than me ...' Who?

4 If Grant is 'the Cat', what's his profession?

5 Who played *His Girl Friday* in a newsdesk comedy of rat-a-tat over-lapping wisecracks?

6 Where was Grant born, with what name?

7 You ain't had ham if you ain't had ... what?

8 Which male western star was Grant reputed to have had an affair with?

9 Who done Grant wrong?

10 Where, if you want to, can you see Grant in drag and in uniform?

11 Name the gossip queen who showed up for the supernatural comedy *Topper*.

12 Who was Grant's leading lady in *To Catch a Thief*?

★ 'Uncle Leo's bedtime story for you older tots! The things they do among the playful rich – oh, boy!' The society comedy?

TB When a journalist sent the telegram, 'How old Cary Grant?', how did Grant reply?

[50]
MODEL ANIMATION

(S) Ermintrude, Florence and Zebedee. The children's TV series?

1 Who made *Tulips Shall Grow* in 1942, the tale of Holland being over-run by Nazi-like mechanical soldiers?

2 'What's this? They're busy throwing snowballs instead of throwing heads.' Christmas Town takes Jack Skellington by surprise in which virtuoso feature?

3 *Conversation Pieces, Next, War Story, Wallace and Gromit*. The Bristol studio?

4 How does the penguin villain of *The Wrong Trousers* disguise himself?

5 Who was Todd Armstrong playing when he battled with Ray Harryhausen's skeletons?

6 Which silent comic began *The Three Ages* riding on a clay dinosaur?

7 Who animated the original *King Kong*?

8 On whose short story is the Brothers Quay's *Street of Crocodiles* based?

9 What's the name of the villainous dog in *A Close Shave*?

10 Whose *Alice* entered Wonderland by crawling into the drawer of a table in a wasteland?

11 Whose plasticine friends are Wendy, Bob and Vince?

12 Whose satire tells of a sculptor forced by a tyrannical Hand to sculpt his likeness for a monument?

★ In which Brothers Quay film does a doll leave its hands hanging from a ladder?

TB What is Wallace's favourite kind of cheese?

[51]

THAT EALING FEELING

(S) Alec Guinness, Stanley Holloway, Sid James, Alfie Bass. Known to the police as …?

1 Who oversaw film-making at MGM-British, Gainsborough, Gaumont-British and other studios, but will be best remembered for such Ealing films as *Passport to Pimlico*, *The Man in the White Suit* and *Whisky Galore*?

2 What great advantage did the Londoners of *Passport to Pimlico* find in declaring themselves part of Burgundy?

3 How many members of the D'Ascoyne clan did Alec Guinness play in *Kind Hearts and Coronets*?

4 What happened at the end of *The Ladykillers*, when Miss Lop-sided told the police all about the stolen loot?

5 By what time-honoured gambit did Alec Guinness escape from a guarded room in *The Man in the White Suit*?

6 Which branch line locomotive was threatened with closure by faceless rail mandarins, in a film which typified Ealing's sympathy for the small community standing up against the powers that be?

7 Which Monsarrat tale of a wartime Atlantic corvette provided an untypical Ealing enterprise?

8 A patient foresees a disastrous bus crash in a dream. A ventriloquist is terrorised by his sadistic dummy. A hellish world is seen through a looking-glass. And a meek man finds himself caught in a recurring nightmare. Which 1945 film?

9 What is Guinness's final thought in *The Man in the White Suit*?

10 Where does Will Hay find himself up Big Ben, as a villain bumps off those responsible for landing him in prison?

11 What did Sandy Mackendrick make sure there was no shortage of for John Gregson, Basil Radford, Gordon Jackson and James Robertson Justice?

12 Who was *Scott of the Antarctic*?

★ Who wrote *The Man in the White Suit*, as well as many of Ealing's other finest?

TB In which wartime film did George Formby inflict his ukulele music on the people of Bergen?

∪SIC FOR MOVIES

S Do the spaceships of *2001: A Space Odyssey* foxtrot, tango or waltz?

1 Who gave *Jaws* its dun-dun-dun-dun-dun?

2 What story did *Fantasia* set to Stravinsky's *The Rite of Spring*?

3 'Farewell, mein lieber Herr, It was a grand affair, But now it's over!' The film?

4 Which composer links the sweeping scores for *Chariots of Fire*, *Blade Runner* and *1492: Conquest of Paradise*?

5 If it's post-war Vienna, and Harry Lime is in the vicinity, what's the musical instrument?

6 Did *Birth of a Nation* and *Intolerance* have musical scores?

7 Where can you see *Pink Elephants on Parade*?

8 Who joined the French Foreign Legion, gained a fortune, lost a leg, and wrote scores for *Anything Goes* and *Kiss Me Kate*?

9 *Vertigo*, *North by Northwest*, *Taxi Driver*. The composer?

10 Which hit musical was inspired by a TV series inspired by a film inspired by the golden age of rock 'n' roll?

11 What's *The Self-Preservation Society*'s preferred mode of transport?

12 Who struggled in voiceover to describe *Manhattan* as Gershwin's *Rhapsody in Blue* played?

★ Who had a musical duel with a hillbilly youth in *Deliverance*?

TB Who created the atmospheric score for *The Last Temptation of Christ* with a range of Middle Eastern musicians?

[53]

LAUREL AND HARDY

(S) What part of his clothing did Oliver Hardy fiddle with at his most apologetically pompous?

1 At the beginning of *Blockheads* (1938), what important piece of information about the First World War hadn't been passed to Stan?

2 In *Way Out West*, why did Stan finish singing *The Trail of the Lonesome Pine* in falsetto?

3 Who perfected the moustache-bristling double-take as the stooge of many of Stan and Ollie's films?

4 Which of the pair was born Arthur Jefferson in Lancashire?

5 In which film did the boys play sailors causing an escalating traffic jam?

6 Who or what was *Laughing Gravy*?

7 Which of the two stayed behind after the day's shooting to work on the gags, while the other went off to play golf?

8 Where in the world were they when desperately trying to find a live grenade in a heap of grenades?

9 What is it about Stan and Ollie's (and for that matter Morecambe and Wise's) on-screen sleeping habits might today be misconstrued?

10 Who were Stan and Ollie when they played their own offspring in an oversized nursery?

11 Why were the boys unhappy that they had been filmed roistering as *Sons of the Desert*?

12 What kind of breakfast did Stan and Ollie prepare for the villain in *Saps at Sea*?

★ 'Mr Hardy holds that a man should always tell his wife the whole truth. Mr Laurel is crazy too.' Which film?

TB When asked, 'You never met my wife, did you?', what did Stan reply?

[54]
EDITING

(5) A burning treeline. Helicopters. Cut to a hotel fan. The film?

1   Who (or so the story goes) discovered editing's potential for trickery when a camera jam caused a lorry to seemingly transform itself into a hearse?

2   What is a pic-sync?

3   In *Citizen Kane*'s opening sequence, which moves closer, shot by shot, to Kane's mansion, what element remains in the same place in all of the shots?

4   Who edited *Pygmalion* and *49th Parallel*?

5   A fade-in superimposed over a fade-out makes a what?

6   Who, with his assistant Grigori Alexandrov, developed montage, a way of generating a new third meaning from the cutting together of two shots?

7   What happens if the 180° Rule is broken in a scene of two actors talking face to face?

8   What is an Academy leader?

9   How was Omar Sharif's entrance in *Lawrence of Arabia* improved for the Director's Cut?

10 In *The Silence of the Lambs*, what surprise does the editing store up for us when Jodie Foster is in Buffalo Bill's house, and the FBI are gathering outside?

11 What kind of fakery do documentary makers employ to allow an interviewee's account to be edited without the jarring effect of jump-cuts?

12 What is a chinagraph pencil used for?

★   How did audiences react when Lev Kuleshov showed them different sequences, where the same shot of an actor's face was intercut with different emotionally-charged shots?

TB 'George has an internal time-clock that he cuts to,' says George's assistant, Duwayne Dunham. 'As soon as a shot becomes boring, bingo! You're out of there!' George who?

[55]
BIBLICAL EPICS

(5) Who has played Moses, John the Baptist, Mark Antony and Michelangelo?

1 'The oldest trick in the world. Silk trap, baited with a woman.' Who talking about whom?

2 For which film was a water set dyed Mediterranean blue, and an extra who fell in and turned blue was kept on the MGM payroll until it wore off?

3 Who played *Salome* to Alan Badel's John the Baptist and Stewart Granger's Commander Claudius?

4 What happens to the image when Christ (Willem Dafoe) dies in *The Last Temptation of Christ*?

5 Which character has been played by Ian McShane, Harvey Keitel, David McCallum and Rip Torn?

6 And which character by José Ferrer, Christopher Plummer, Josh Mostel and Charles Laughton?

7 Who cut *Exodus* (set during the birth of modern Israel) to such a length that at the premiere Mort Sahl stood up and said, 'Otto, let my people go'?

8 Who said of *Samson and Delilah*, 'It's the first picture I've seen in which the male lead has bigger tits than the female'?

9 To whom did Quintus Arrius say, 'Your eyes are full of hate, forty-one. That's good. Hate keeps a man alive'?

10 What role did Yul Brynner play in *The Ten Commandments*?

11 Who, when the producers of the much-delayed *Quo Vadis* told him he might be too young to play Nero, replied, 'If you wait much longer I shall be too old. Nero died at thirty-one'?

12 Who played Pontius Pilate in *The Last Temptation of Christ*?

★ In what language did Robert Aldrich make *The Last Days of Sodom and Gomorrah*?

TB Who co-wrote *Intolerance* with D. W. Griffith, though he is best known for directing *Freaks*?

[56]
FRITZ LANG

(S) Who played Maria and the Robot in *Metropolis*?

1   'I can't help myself! I haven't any control over this evil thing that's inside me ...' Lang's mother, having nightmares about the child in her womb, Peter Lorre's murderer explaining himself in *M*, or Lang confessing to his bullying of actors?

2   In which film do Edward G. Robinson and Joan Bennett try to conceal a killing?

3   And how does Robinson commit this killing (in self-defence)?

4   In *Metropolis*'s message, what is supposed to 'mediate between the head and the hands'?

5   What film format did Lang dismiss as 'only good for funerals and snakes'?

6   When (supposedly) Lang said, 'My mother had Jewish parents', what was Joseph Goebbels' reply?

7   What, in English, are *Die Tausend Augen des Dr Mabuse*?

8   In which film is an innocent Spencer Tracy terrorised by a lynch-mob?

9   Which columnist observed of the work Lang's wife did on his behalf, 'There's a man who got where he is by the sweat of his Frau'?

10 Who collaborated with Lang on the script of *Hangmen Also Die*?

11 What drives Arthur Kennedy to Marlene Dietrich's *Rancho Notorious*?

12 Why is Peter Lorre caught in *M*?

★   Which film did Lang's involvement in *The Spiders* (1919–20) prevent him from directing?

TB Who was Paul Richter when he slew the dragon?

[57]

HOLLYWOOD
AFTER *STAR WARS*

(S) 1982's updating of *The Thing from Another World* (or *Alien* in the Antarctic). The Kurt Russell film?

1   What criticism is most often (with some justification) levelled at the trend *Star Wars* set for Hollywood movie-making?

2   Which luridly coloured saga had the *Fiddler on the Roof* building a space rocket and James Bond ruling an arboreal world?

3   What did *Battlestar Galactica* have instead of stormtroopers?

4   In *Star Trek: The Motion Picture*, who or what was VGER?

5   Which Japanese classic is spoofed in *Battle Beyond the Stars*?

6   What's the difference between the ways that the Terminators are animated in *The Terminator* and *T2: Judgement Day*?

7   Which was the only film to out-gross the re-released *Star Wars* at the box office in 1997?

8   Which *Star Wars* actor has provided the voice of The Joker?

9   Which Jeff Bridges film was the first feature to attempt a comprehensively computer-generated world?

10 Who has been Hollywood's favourite technoboffin in *The Fly*, *Jurassic Park* and *Independence Day*?

11 Which *Star Wars* trilogy characters had their own spin-off called *Caravan of Courage*?

12 Which branch of Lucas's empire makes computer games?

★   Who or what connects Ewan McGregor to the first *Star Wars* trilogy?

TB What George Lucas flop was christened *Howard the Turkey*?

[58]

CASABLANCA

⑤ Does *Casablanca* conclude in a casbah, a police station, a Moorish fort or an airport?

1 What government did Claude Rains' Captain Renault represent?

2 'Ilse, I'm no good at being noble, but it doesn't take much to see that the problems of three little people don't amount to ...' What?

3 '*Reek, Reek*, you've got to hide me ...' The marvellous saucer-eyed actor?

4 Who menaced as Major Strasser, after a career of Germanic darkness in films like *Caligari* and *Waxworks*?

5 What documents central to the plot were invented by writers Julius and Philip Epstein and Howard Koch?

6 Who sang *As Time Goes By* and *Knock on Wood*?

7 By chance, *Casablanca* was given added resonance by which real wartime event?

8 Who might have been Rick, but had to settle for President?

9 Why was it so imperative that Victor (Paul Henreid) get passage away to America?

10 No matter what happened, Rick and Ilsa would always have ... where?

11 Name another movie which featured Bogart, Lorre and Sydney Greenstreet.

12 Why in one scene do lattice bar shadows fall across Rick and his black and white striped tie?

★ *Casablanca*'s light and shadows mark a transition from the style of the pre-war gangster movies to the post-war *films noirs*, for which studio?

TB Why did Rick say he had come to Casablanca?

[59]

ROBERT DE NIRO

(S) 'Are you talkin' to me?' The film?

1 For which director has De Niro played hoodlums, a boxer, a vigilante and a failed stand-up comic?

2 How did Al Capone dispatch one of his henchmen at a board meeting in *The Untouchables*?

3 Who played the pimp who took some killing in *Taxi Driver*?

4 Which film brought De Niro and Keitel to fame as young New York hoods?

5 Who was Louis Cypher really, and in which film?

6 What kind of robbery made Eddie Conway paranoid in *Goodfellas*?

7 Where did Al Pacino star in a first film, and De Niro in the sequel?

8 And where did they meet face to face, as a cop and an armed robber?

9 Which sprawling saga of gangster lives from the twenties to the sixties starred De Niro, James Woods and Elizabeth McGovern?

10 What death couldn't De Niro save Christopher Walken from in *The Deer Hunter*?

11 What style of acting did De Niro exemplify in *Raging Bull*, where he learned to box and put on 50 pounds in weight?

12 In which film did De Niro play a patient emerging from a catatonic illness?

★ Which character gave a false address to a secret serviceman at a political rally?

TB Who did De Niro threaten with fistophobia if he didn't overcome his fear of planes?

[60]
HAROLD LLOYD

(S) What kind of lenses were in the Glasses Character's glasses?

1　In which film does Lloyd's hypochondriac sleepwalk through a banana republic revolution?

2　In the same film, how does he befriend the giant?

3　In which film does Lloyd dangle from *that* clock?

4　And what forced him to climb up there in the first place?

5　How did Lloyd lose the thumb and forefinger of his right hand?

6　In 1949 Lloyd was elected Imperial Potentate of what organisation?

7　Who is Lloyd when, striving for popularity, he volunteers to be a tackle-dummy for a college football squad?

8　Who climbed higher and higher up a tree to keep his departing love in view?

9　Why doesn't the villain brain the Kid Brother when he clubs him on the head in the derelict ship?

10　Why did much of *Welcome Danger* have to be re-shot?

11　Who did Lloyd work for at the Rolin Film Company?

12　What does Lloyd career through city streets on a horse-drawn wagon to prevent? In which film?

★　Name the two major characters that Lloyd used before settling on the Glasses Character.

TB　Did Lloyd receive an Honorary Oscar ('To Harold Lloyd – Master Comedian and Good Citizen') in 1942, 1952 or 1962?

[61]

SERGEI EISENSTEIN

(S) Which famous sequence in *The Battleship Potemkin* cross-cuts between advancing soldiers and the ordinary people suffering under their fire?

1 What method of editing a film did Eisenstein almost single-handedly invent?

2 Was Eisenstein born in Russia, Latvia, the Ukraine or Germany?

3 Which Russian hero did Eisenstein depict battling the Teutonic Knights on a frozen lake?

4 Who photographed *Potemkin* and most of Eisenstein's other works?

5 Which film intercuts sequences of a cream separator and a virile bull to show off Soviet productivity?

6 And which film contrasts the slaughter of a bull with a massacre of workers by Tsarist troops?

7 How is meaning created in a montage sequence?

8 Whose life was documented, in two parts and partly in colour, at the end of Eisenstein's career?

9 After the Civil War, which theatre did Eisenstein join: the White Army Theatre, the Proletkult Theatre, the Bolshoi or the Old Vic?

10 Which unfinished film was shot in Mexico, detailing peasant life and including scenes of the local Death Day?

11 Eisenstein visited Hollywood, and encountered such heroes of the revolution as Mickey Mouse. True or false?

12 What piece of colour tinting concludes *Potemkin*?

★ Who was Eisenstein's assistant before going on to direct *Circus* and *Volga-Volga*?

TB Who composed the music for *Alexander Nevsky*?

[62]

THE FRENCH NEW WAVE

(S) What does *A Bout de Souffle* mean?

1 In what cold future city did Jean-Luc Godard land Eddie Constantine?

2 Oskar Werner and Jeanne Moreau starred in which François Truffaut film of 1962?

3 Rebelling against the French received wisdom that the writer, adapting classic works of literature, was the most important party in the film-making process, who did the New Wave hold up as the film's creative hero?

4 Which Claude Chabrol film, about a student trying to set his friend on the straight and narrow, is reckoned to have started the New Wave?

5 What was Louis Malle's *Zazie dans le Métro* about?

6 Who directed *Pauline at the Beach* and *Ma Nuit Chez Maud*?

7 A Jewish schoolboy tried to hide his identity from the Nazis in which 1988 Malle film?

8 Who was the beast of Chabrol's *The Beast Must Die*?

9 Which famous film magazine is most closely associated with the New Wave?

10 When and where might Giorgio Albertazzi and Delphine Seyrig have met before?

11 What part of which girl's anatomy was Jean-Claude Brialy obsessed by?

12 Which grand old thesp had strange reminiscences of his sons and their wives in Alan Resnais's *Providence*?

★ Who photographed Truffaut's *Fahrenheit 451*, and went on to notably direct Julie Christie himself?

TB Brits like Albert Finney, John Osborne, Tom Courtenay and Richard Burton made up which roughly equivalent group across the water?

[63]

BETTE DAVIS

(S) 'Oh Jenny, don't let's ask for the moon – when we have the stars.' The picture?

1 Which Southern belle vehicle did Davis ride in part due to the success of *Gone with the Wind*, the novel?

2 Who was Davis's high-hairlined *Virgin Queen*?

3 'Fasten your seat belts; it's going to be a bumpy night.' The movie?

4 What adaptation from a Lillian Hellman play had Davis agonising over whether to kill her husband to get the money for a partnership in a cotton mill?

5 Which of her leading men said, 'I've been close to Bette Davis for thirty-eight years – and I have the cigarette burns to prove it'?

6 Whose scruffiness, which was to help make him a greater star than her, did Davis complain about in memos during *The Petrified Forest*?

7 Who said in *All About Eve*, 'I am a critic and a commentator. I am essential to the theatre – as ants to a picnic, as the boll weevil to a cotton field'?

8 Which superior flake of soap was based on the Olive Higgins novel, and had Paul Henreid lighting his and Davis's cigarettes in his mouth at once?

9 Which brash young male did Davis resent getting top billing in *The Sisters*?

10 Where did Davis play a dying heiress alongside Bogart, George Brent and Ronald Reagan?

11 What accent did Davis have to master for *Of Human Bondage*?

12 'When my cleaning man heard Joan and I were co-starring [in *Whatever Happened to Baby Jane*?], he suggested we shoot the picture in the Coliseum.' Joan who?

★ According to Louella Parsons, you don't carry on a conversation with Davis, you . . . what?

TB Who had Davis imagined as Essex to her Elizabeth, rather than Errol Flynn?

[64]

THE RISE AND
RISE OF HOLLYWOOD

(S) What name for early American film theatres derived from the admission charge?

1 Who directed *The Great Train Robbery* in 1903?

2 What organisation, formed in 1908, imposed strict quotas on the number of foreign films shown in America?

3 Although Hollywood became synonymous with the film industry, in which city were most of the studio head offices?

4 What term was given to the task of editing the shots of a film so that they appeared smooth and comprehensible to the audience?

5 Who had four legs and helped to establish Warner Bros?

6 What event caused European production companies to drastically lose ground to the young Hollywood, or cease production altogether?

7 Name three of the four historical settings of D. W. Griffith's *Intolerance*.

8 What was block booking?

9 Was the Hays Code imposed on Hollywood by the film industry itself, by the Los Angeles City Council or by the US Government?

10 What was controversial about Cecil B. de Mille's *King of Kings*?

11 Written by General Lew Wallace, and given a lavish MGM adaptation in 1926. The epic tale?

12 Phonofilm, Movietone, Photophone and Vitaphone were all early examples of what?

★ What's the difference between tinting and toning a black and white print?

TB Who lit a cigarette with a smoking anarchist bomb in *Cops*?

[65]

KIRK DOUGLAS

(S) What began with a gladiator trainer being drowned in a pot of broth?

1   What was the *Ace in the Hole* for Douglas's unscrupulous journalist?

2   What was killing Doc Holliday as surely as any bullet?

3   Is Douglas's real name (a) Walter Matasschanskayasky, (b) Herbert ze Schluderpacheru, (c) Larushka Mischa Skikne, or (d) Issur Danielovitch Demsky?

4   In which war did the *Paths of Glory* lead to the grave?

5   Where did Douglas have to contend with a kraken, a futuristic submarine and James Mason's definitive Captain Nemo?

6   Who had a *Lust for Life*: (a) Michelangelo, (b) Van Gogh, (c) Rembrandt or (d) Rolf Harris?

7   Who built a robot that menaced Douglas and Farrah Fawcett in *Saturn Three*?

8   Who has been Douglas's comrade in Roman and Viking times?

9   In what sport was Douglas a doomed *Champion*?

10 What is the premise of *Seven Days in May*?

11 In which TV series did son Michael Douglas make his name?

12 Who was the private eye hired by Douglas's gangster to find his mistress?

★   How was Anthony Quinn connected to the rape and murder of Douglas's wife in *Last Train from Gun Hill*?

TB 'My kids never had the advantage I had,' says Douglas. What advantage?

[66]
PSYCHO

(**S**) At which motel is it advisable to keep on driving?

1 Why is Janet Leigh's Marion Crane so nervous when the highway cop questions her?

2 And why does she trade her car in?

3 Why does Norman Bates (Anthony Perkins) offer Marion Cabin 1?

4 What hobby of Norman's is on display in his parlour?

5 Who is 'a boy's best friend'?

6 What surname links Marion's boyfriend with Donald Pleasance's shrink in *Halloween*?

7 What does Norman do with Marion's body?

8 How does Arbogast the private investigator (Martin Balsam) die?

9 Who plays Marion's sister?

10 What psychological process led to Marion's murder?

11 What do they find in the cellar?

12 Ee-ee-ee-ee! Who made the violins scream?

★ Whose gruesome real-life killings inspired *Psycho* (among others)?

TB What happens to Norman's face in the police cell?

[67]
WALT DISNEY

(S) *Genuflect, show some respect, for Prince Ali! … Who was Prince Ali really?*

1 Who accidentally got drunk and imagined *Pink Elephants on Parade*?

2 What name did the young King Arthur answer to in *The Sword in the Stone*?

3 Conceived as a mix of buffalo, lion and gorilla, who am I?

4 Who first appeared in the 1928 short *Steamboat Willie*?

5 Name all Seven Dwarfs.

6 And Donald Duck's nephews?

7 Where are the world's four Disney theme parks?

8 What job did Jimminy Cricket do for Pinocchio?

9 What Tim Burton tale, produced in 1993 by Disney's Touchstone wing, provided a very alternative vision to the mainstream Disney look?

10 Whose song, *The Circle of Life*, was bombastic enough to win the Best Song Oscar for *The Lion King*?

11 *Toccata and Fugue. The Sorcerer's Apprentice. Night on the Bare Mountain. The, er, Pastoral Symphony.* The flawed masterpiece?

12 What creatures were *The Hunchback of Notre Dame*'s obligatory side-kicks?

★ What was unusual about the wildlife documentary *The Living Desert*?

TB What was Disney's original name for Mickey?

[68]
THE DOCUMENTARY

(S) Who first seduced the world with the wonder of the *cinématograph* by holding screenings across five continents?

1 Which early American documentarist yearned for unspoilt places, where civilisation hadn't yet eroded the lifestyles of people like *Nanook of the North*?

2 Which Ken Burns series of 1990 wove archive photographs, eye-witness narratives and a gem of a raconteur into an emotional fabric which made it something of a national event in the US?

3 What service was celebrated in a 1936 British film that clacked along to a W. H. Auden poem and a Benjamin Britten score?

4 Which Dziga Vertov film documented a day in the life of a Soviet city, as well as the process of film-making, and even included an animation of the camera assembling itself and walking away on its tripod?

5 What were the two sequels to David Attenborough's *Life on Earth*?

6 Making himself a documentary expert in double-quick time, Frank Capra produced what series of films explaining to conscripts the purpose of the War against Germany and Japan?

7 *Night Mail* was born from out of the assembled talents of the General Post Office (GPO) Film Unit. Who was the Unit's head?

8 CBS's *The Selling of the Pentagon* highlighted the many ways in which the US Military was preaching participation in which conflict?

9 What was the *Turksib* documented in 1929 by Victor Turin?

10 Who in Britain took a quieter, more lyrical approach to the wartime propaganda movie than the more tub-thumping morale raisers, in such films as *Listen to Britain* and *Fires Were Started*?

11 In which series did Kenneth Clark guide us along the course of Western Art, setting a trend for epic, personality-centred educations?

12 Who were the two Presidential candidates who allowed Richard Leacock unprecedented access to their campaigns, for *Primary* (1960)?

★ Who documented American institutions in the sixties and seventies, for example in *Titicut Follies* and *Basic Training*?

TB Who stood up to McCarthyism in CBS's *See it Now* series?

[69]

GONE WITH THE WIND

(5) Which city burns?

1 'Forget it, Louis, no Civil War picture ever made a nickel.' Irving Thalberg advising whom?

2 Who wrote the blockbuster novel?

3 True or false: one Scarlett wannabe had herself gift-wrapped and delivered to David O. Selznick's house?

4 Why did Clark Gable stress the 'give' in 'Frankly my dear, I don't give a damn'?

5 'Miss Scarlett, I don't know nothin' bout birthin' babies!' The character?

6 What was the age difference between Vivien Leigh and Barbara O'Neil, who played her mother: a year, 5 years, 45 or 55 years?

7 Who could have co-starred in a package with Bette Davis, except Davis refused because he was too much of a womaniser?

8 Where did Scarlett first enquire about Rhett: at the Twelve Oaks barbecue, the Seven Cedars dance or the Nine Elms ball?

9 Who played Ashley Wilkes?

10 Name the three who share the directors' credit.

11 And which of the three was fired by Selznick only 10 days into the production?

12 Rhett boasted to Scarlett that he could drill a dime at ... 20, 50 or 70 yards?

★ Who was Frank Kennedy engaged to before he married Scarlett?

TB What was Scarlett's final consolation?

[70]
BILLY WILDER

(S) In *Some Like it Hot*, whose lines did Wilder have to paste inside a set of drawers?

1 With which Hungarian actor did Wilder share an apartment after coming to Hollywood?

2 What's the last line of *Sunset Boulevard*?

3 In what way does Ray Milland lose *The Lost Weekend*?

4 'Lately you've begun to imagine in Cinemascope … with stereophonic sound.' Tom Ewell's fantasy in which film?

5 Who has a cameo appearance in *Sunset Boulevard*: Charlie Chaplin, Buster Keaton, Fatty Arbuckle or Harold Lloyd?

6 What is Wilder's country of birth?

7 In *Some Like it Hot*, who does Tony Curtis impersonate as he plays the playboy?

8 And who (any resemblance to real life being purely coincidental) plays the Mob boss out to get Curtis and Lemmon?

9 When unable to obtain the bidet his wife requested, what did Wilder, by telegram, suggest?

10 In which film does Fred MacMurray say, 'Do I laugh now, or wait till it gets funny?'?

11 Who was the *Witness for the Prosecution*?

12 What was the next black and white film to win the Best Picture Oscar after *The Apartment*?

★ 'I have ten commandments,' said Wilder. 'The first nine are thou shalt not bore. The tenth is …' What?

TB What was Wilder's credit for *Ninotchka*?

[71]
SCIENCE FICTION

(5) Created by Alex Raymond. Played by Buster Crabbe. Who am I?

1 Who brought a magician's expertise to cinema at the turn of the century, and became the father of special effects and science fiction films?

2 And what was Fritz Lang's profession prior to film directing, shown to good effect in *Metropolis*'s vast vision of a future society?

3 Who loved LUH 3417?

4 'We'll start with a few murders. Big men, little men – just to show we make no distinction.' Which vision of a scientist gone mad?

5 What Thing was likened to an intellectual carrot?

6 A global war around 1940. Ruins and unrest. Raymond Massey. A future society launching a Moon rocket. Which piece of prophecy?

7 Who are David Bowman and Frank Poole?

8 On what play was *Forbidden Planet* based?

9 If Eldin Tyrrell designs replicants, who has to hunt them down if they run amok?

10 What kind of movements did the model spaceships in *Star Wars* have to perform?

11 Which 1956 film, starring Kevin McCarthy and aliens who emerged from pods to impersonate humans, was taken as a metaphor for 'reds under the beds' paranoia?

12 Apart from Jones the cat, who was the only survivor of the *Nostromo*? In which film?

★ In which Tarkovsky film does a psychically charged planet haunt the characters with ghosts from their pasts?

TB What day was it when Michael Rennie encountered a giant silver spacefarer, who warned the world to end its wars?

[72]

WHO SAID ...?

Name the characters (or actors) who spoke these lines, and the films in which they spoke them.

S 'Saigon. *Shit.*'

1 'Rest easy son, you've had a busy day.'

2 'Only two kinds of creatures get fun in the desert: Bedouins and gods, and you're neither.'

3 'Please, could you give me a glass of water? I've got something in my eye and I want to bathe it.'

4 'It's injustice I hate, not the Normans.'

5 'Hang on lads, I've got a great idea. Uh ... uh ...'

6 'I distrust a man who says when. He's got to be careful not to drink too much, because he's not to be trusted when he does.'

7 'I'm sorry Dave, I can't do that.'

8 'We did lose a million dollars last year. We expect to lose a million next year, too. You know, Mr Thatcher – at the rate of a million a year – we'll have to close this place – in sixty years.'

9 'You gonna bark all day, little doggie, or are you gonna bite?'

10 'I've seen things you people wouldn't believe. Attack ships on fire off the shoulder of Orion. I watched C-beams glitter in the dark near Tannhäuser Gate. All those moments will be lost in time, like tears in rain. Time to die.'

11 'Mein Führer! I can walk!'

12 'I'm talkin' about friendship. I'm talkin' about character. I'm talkin' about – hell, Leo, I ain't embarrassed to use the word – I'm talkin' about ethics.'

★ 'The prettiest sight in this fine pretty world is the privileged class enjoying its privileges.'

TB '*Beee gooood ...*'

[73]

INGMAR BERGMAN

(S) With whom does Max von Sydow's knight play chess in *The Seventh Seal*?

1 Name the former silent director who plays the dour academic protagonist of *Wild Strawberries*.

2 And who played both his past sweetheart and a present-day girl who hitches a ride with him?

3 The knight returns from the Crusades to find what other great slayer of people?

4 Who based his musical *A Little Night Music* on *Smiles of a Summer Night*?

5 Was Bergman's father a chaplain to the Swedish Royal Family, a mortician, or the inventor of a brand of antidepressant?

6 Which film charts the relationship between a traumatised actress and the nurse who cares for her?

7 What is the name of Bergman's 1987 autobiography?

8 Which film portrays three women during a fateful two days in a maternity ward?

9 When their actor-manager father dies, who find themselves the stepchildren of an austere clergyman?

10 What happened to Bergman in 1976 which led to him having a nervous breakdown?

11 In which film does a painter on an island descend into madness?

12 Name either the actress who played a dying sister, or the actress who played a suicidal sister, in *Cries and Whispers*.

★ Of Bergman's two regular cameramen, Sven Nykvist is the best-known. Who is the other?

TB What won the Best Foreign Film Oscar for 1962?

[74]
PULP FICTION

(S) Who tries to turn from being 'the tyranny of evil men' to being a shepherd?

1   And which book of the Bible is he quoting from?

2   As Marsellus (Ving Rhames) says to Butch (Bruce Willis), what goes down in the fifth?

3   What does the poppa tomato say to the dawdling baby tomato?

4   Why does Lance (Eric Stoltz) search desperately for his black medical book?

5   What are Tim Roth's and Amanda Plummer's nicknames for each other?

6   What do they put on french fries in Holland instead of ketchup?

7   Who has a list that reads:
1265 Riverside Drive
Toluca Lake
1 body (no head)
Bloody shot-up car
Jules (black)
Vincent (Dean Martin)
Jimmie (house)
Bonnie (9:30)

8   Why did Marsellus have Antwan Rockamora killed?

9   How was Jules's hair originally intended to look?

10 Who wouldn't you ever want to go to the toilet when you were around?

11 With what two items are Marsellus and his friends going to 'go to work' on Zed with?

12 What does Jules think was an act of divine intervention?

★   What was Mia's speciality in the TV show Fox Force Five?

TB Mia claims that everyone can be classified as one of two types of person. What types?

[75]
CLINT EASTWOOD

(**S**) 'I don't think it's nice you laughin' ...' Which iconic Western?

1 Which Western TV series brought Eastwood to the public's attention as Rowdy Yates?

2 Who showcased his larger-than-life visual style to good effect in Eastwood's Spaghetti Westerns, and later in epics such as *Once Upon a Time in America*?

3 In which film did Eastwood play a DJ stalked by a crazed female fan?

4 Who painted a town red (literally) to announce to the bad guys that they were entering hell?

5 What was the great blemish on Eastwood's professional past in the disappointing *In the Line of Fire*?

6 In real life, Eastwood served as mayor of which Californian town?

7 What was the name of Eastwood's character in *A Fistful of Dollars*?

8 Who carried a .44 Magnum, chased the villain's phone calls from booth to booth, and gave us 'Do you feel lucky, punk?'

9 What was the real aim of Eastwood's and Richard Burton's mission in *Where Eagles Dare*?

10 Whose nemesis was a villainous Unionist 'Redshank' in a Western that sought to redress many Hollywood untruths about the West?

11 In which film did Eastwood see a fellow inmate chop off his fingers because his painting privileges had been withdrawn?

12 In which atrocious 1982 film did Eastwood steal a top secret Soviet plane?

★ In *Unforgiven*, what dilemma did the scarred prostitute present Will Munney when she offered to sleep with him?

TB Who was Clyde?

[76]

THE MARCH
OF TECHNOLOGY

S What is a subwoofer?

1 Who in 1889 invented perforated celluloid film?

2 Why do people walk too quickly in early silent footage?

3 How, in October 1927, did Warner Brothers, one of Hollywood's smaller studios, strengthen their position in the industry?

4 Give a reason why talkies were for a few years static affairs, the camera rooted to the spot in comparison with the final achievements of the silent era.

5 What colour process was devised by Daniel Comstock and Herbert Kalmus, first as a two, then a three, colour system?

6 What was the prime advantage of replacing film's old cellulose-nitrate base with cellulose acetate?

7 Where on the film strip is the Dolby SR-D soundtrack printed?

8 What kind of camera harness allows the camera operator to walk and run while maintaining a smooth, level shot?

9 Which domestic video format had the better picture quality: VHS or Betamax?

10 And what does VHS stand for?

11 In what area of film technology has John Lasseter been a pioneer for a decade and more?

12 Why has Hollywood been keen to have different standards of the new Digital Video Disc technology implemented in different regions of the world?

★ How does the Dykstraflex motion control system make it easier to add special effects to a shot?

TB What does an anamorphic lens do?

[77]
HORROR

(S) What did Buffalo Bill's victims in *The Silence of the Lambs* have stuck in their throats?

1 Bald, pointy-eared, and chillingly cadaverous, plague rats followed him wherever he went. Which German classic?

2 When did Michael Myers and Jason become monsters behind their masks?

3 What name is given to the twisted and exaggerated scenery and lighting of dark early German classics like *The Cabinet of Doctor Caligari*?

4 *Night of the Living Dead. Creepshow. Hungry Wives.* The director?

5 Where did Melvyn Douglas, Charles Laughton, Raymond Massey and Boris Karloff find themselves in 1932?

6 What night might it be if you willingly accepted a slip of paper marked with runes?

7 Who rode to young superstardom on a tide of green vomit?

8 Is Polanski's *Repulsion* the story of (a) a Belgian manicurist who becomes increasingly paranoid, (b) the frictions between two ageing Hollywood sisters, or (c) a young Polish man's infatuation with a woman in the opposite flat?

9 Which modern Italian director's shockers include *Inferno* and *The Bird with Crystal Plumage*?

10 Which James Whale film, starring Elsa Lanchester as both the title character and the original author, is often voted the best horror movie of all?

11 *Freddy's Revenge, Dream Warriors* and *Freddy's Dead: The Final Nightmare* are sequels to what?

12 Who shot to fame in 1931 with lines like 'Listen to the creatures of the night. What music they make!'?

★ What did a Jewish Rabbi in Prague create to protect his people from persecution?

TB Who has filmed exploding heads, a talking bottom, a gynaecologist dissecting his twin, and folk who enjoy car accidents a bit more than they should?

[78]

THE STUDIO SYSTEM

(S) Name three of the four people who founded United Artists in 1919

1 Which studio boasted that it had 'more stars than there are in heaven'?

2 What does RKO stand for?

3 Name any four of the so-called 'Big Five' studios of the thirties.

4 And any two of the 'Small Three' of the same period.

5 Which studio produced *Dracula, Frankenstein* and *The Invisible Man*?

6 Which genre began with *Twentieth Century* and *It Happened One Night*?

7 Whose biggest stars in the thirties included Will Rogers and Shirley Temple?

8 What did a Supreme Court decision of 1948 force the Major studios to sell off?

9 What chief competition led to the decline in traditional studio production in the fifties?

10 What new kind of theatre of the fifties was especially convenient for the suburbanised, car-driving American populace?

11 Which studio was owned for a period by Howard Hughes before ceasing production in 1957?

12 Who bought Columbia Pictures in 1982: Coca-Cola, Pepsi, McDonald's or Nabisco?

★ What is a 'vertically integrated' studio?

TB What was MGM's first big success?

[79]
GEORGE LUCAS

(S) What film was conceived with characters called Annikin Starkiller, Mace Windu, Usby C. J. Thape and Leia Aguilae?

1 Which town in Northern California did Lucas grow up in: Fresno, Modesto or Incognito?

2 Why did Lucas's outlook on life change on June 12, 1962?

3 What film was built around four prototypes: the rebel, the solid citizen, the nerd and the king of the road?

4 With which other film did *Star Wars* hold joint casting sessions?

5 *Star Wars* was the first feature to be screened in what sound format?

6 What was the importance of the editor hired from Sadler Films to work with Lucas for the US Information Agency?

7 When shooting *Star Wars*, how did they have to let 'Artoo' know when a shot was cut?

8 Lucas graduated along with John Milius, John Carpenter, Dan O'Bannon and Robert Zemeckis from which college's film school?

9 Why couldn't Lucas shoot any close-ups of Mark Hamill in Death Valley?

10 What is the special effects house that Lucas set up for *Star Wars*, and which has worked on most of Hollywood's blockbusters ever since?

11 What was the main reason why Lucas enjoyed making *Raiders of the Lost Ark* more than any other film?

12 What is the name of the benchmark Lucas has developed for cinema sound quality?

★ Why did Lucas hire a linguist to speak the Inca dialect of Quechua?

TB Who inspired Lucas to grow a full beard?

[80]

SCREENWRITING

(5) Who said to whom, 'You can type this shit, George, but you sure can't say it'?

1 Why did producer Sam Spiegel have to visit a British prison to get the production of *Lawrence of Arabia* back on track?

2 Robert Bolt wasn't executed for his principles. Who was *A Man For All Seasons*, who was?

3 What screenplay did Colin Welland first entitle *Runners*?

4 What does '[beat]' mean in a piece of comedy dialogue?

5 Which John Steinbeck tale did Nunnally Johnson adapt for John Ford?

6 What medical establishment links Ring Lardner Jr and Larry Gelbart, and how?

7 In which firm is the third prize for successful sales the sack? And the writer?

8 What does MCU stand for in a script?

9 Who is pestered by John Goodman while trying to write a wrestling picture?

10 Name the prolific writer who won the Original Story Academy Award at the very first Oscars, and died working on the script for *Casino Royale*.

11 And who sent Hecht a telegram describing working in Hollywood thus: 'Millions are to be grabbed here, and your only competition is idiots. Don't let this get around'?

12 Who inflicted *Sliver*, *Showgirls* and *An Allen Smithee Film* on the world?

★ What is the difference between a Master Scene Script and a Shooting Script?

TB What was unusual about Robert Rich, the Oscar-winning writer of *The Brave One* in 1956?

[81]
THE OSCARS

(S) Who has personally collected more Oscars than anyone else?

1 What aspect of the Oscar statuette's head struck Frances Marian as being symbolic of the movie business?

2 Who is the youngest person to have received the Best Supporting Actress award?

3 And the oldest to win Best Actress?

4 Who won Best Actor and Best Supporting Actor playing the same character in two different movies?

5 Who was the first African American to win a performing Oscar, and in which film?

6 Which family has produced three generations of Oscar-winners?

7 Name two of the three Best Picture westerns

8 Who is the only actor to have directed himself to the Best Actor Oscar?

9 Which actress has been nominated a dozen times?

10 Who is the Academy's most nominated writer?

11 For which Vietnam veteran movie did Jon Voight and Jane Fonda win Best Actor and Best Actress awards?

12 Who was the first person to win an acting award playing a person of the opposite sex?

★ Who won two Oscars in the same year for the same performance?

TB Who are the only brother and sister to have won acting Oscars?

[82]

SATYAJIT RAY

(5) What modern object does Apu first glimpse, wonderstruck, through tall grasses?

1 At which film festival did the West wake up to *Pather Panchali*?

2 What does *Pather Panchali* mean?

3 In which city was Ray born?

4 Which French director met Ray and encouraged him to press on with *Pather Panchali*?

5 What language were almost all of Ray's films made in?

6 Whose play, *An Enemy of the People*, was adapted by Ray in 1989?

7 What are the other films in the Apu trilogy?

8 As *The Chess Players*, Mirza and Mir, sit at their board, what greater game is being played out around them?

9 Which Vittorio de Sica film encouraged Ray to try and shoot *Pather Panchali* on a small budget with nonprofessional actors?

10 How does Apu's wife die?

11 What was Ray's last film, the tale of a family who suspect that a returning prodigal relative may be an impostor?

12 Who provided the sitar music for the Apu trilogy?

★ Name either of the films for which Ray won two Silver Bears in succession at the Berlin Film Festival

TB How does Apu's sister Durga die?

[83]

VIETNAM MOVIES

(S) Who led his Airborne troops into battle to the blared-out sound of *The Ride of the Valkyries*?

1 What euphemistic name was given to bloodsoaked Hill 937, as in the 1987 feature?

2 Name the trilogy of Vietnam films that Oliver Stone began in 1986 on a typically large scale.

3 Who played crippled veteran and campaigner Ron Kovic in *Born on the Fourth of July*?

4 Which 1968 thick-ear effort starred John Wayne and George Takei?

5 What did Private Pile do with his *Full Metal Jacket*s?

6 Which actor was the brother of *The Godfather*, and a buddy of *The Deer Hunter*?

7 What was Jon Voight doing when he fell for Jane Fonda, a soldier's wife?

8 Who respectively played the simply defined Good Sergeant and Bad Sergeant in *Platoon*?

9 What game would Robert De Niro, Christopher Walken and John Savage rather not have played in *The Deer Hunter*?

10 If *First Blood* wasn't gung-ho enough for Reagan's America, what came next?

11 Which unremarkable 1978 effort featured Burt Lancaster?

12 What was intercut with Willard's killing of Colonel Kurtz at the end of *Apocalypse Now*?

★ What happened at My Lai, as examined by Joseph Strick's Oscar-winning documentary, *Interview with My Lai Veterans*?

TB How did Matthew Modine's war trauma exhibit itself in Alan Parker's 1984 outing?

[84]

CITIZEN KANE

(5) What was journalist Thompson trying to find out?

1 *There is a man*
A certain man
And for the poor you may be sure ... Of what?

2 On talking with the leaders of Europe's Great Powers, what was Kane's conclusion?

3 In what line of showbusiness did Kane have his mistress Susan Alexander pushed beyond her ability?

4 What was the name of Kane's pleasurehome?

5 What real newsreel did the *News on the March* sequence satirise?

6 What was the source of the boy Kane's wealth?

7 Who did Orson Welles apparently try to muscle out of the credits list?

8 What was wrong with Kane, and what was wrong with Susan, when they met in the street?

9 Kane began to build his empire around which newspaper?

10 What is the biggest McGuffin in the movie?

11 Which of these Mercury Theatre stalwarts doesn't appear in *Kane*: George Coulouris, John Houseman, Agnes Moorhead or Everett Sloane?

12 What did Kane do with Leland's unfinished slating of Susan's performance?

★ Which European stylistic tradition did photographer Gregg Toland bring from films like *Mad Love*, which strongly influenced the look of *Kane*?

TB Were Kane's first names Cash Flagg, Chester Francis, Chambers Ford or Charles Foster?

[85]
STANLEY KUBRICK

(**5**) 'You can't fight in here – this is the War Room!' Which film?

1 What did Stanley Kubrick manage to sell at age 16, and to whom?

2 What was his first feature-length film?

3 Why did Malcolm McDowell receive a lacerated eye working with Kubrick? In which film?

4 Who hung from a cross on the Appian Way, along with all his followers?

5 In which film does Lee Ermey dish out some of the choicest abuse in cinema?

6 Who did James Mason's Humbert Humbert really want when he married Shelley Winters?

7 Which story of an elaborate racecourse heist gone wrong provided some inspiration for *Reservoir Dogs*?

8 Who claimed he was 'by any practical definition of the words, fool-proof and incapable of error'?

9 What was General Jack D. Ripper's real reason for launching a strike against the Soviets?

10 Which tale of an 18th Century adventurer starred Ryan O'Neal, Steven Berkoff, Hardy Kruger and Leonard Rossiter?

11 Why did Jack Nicholson go berserk in *The Shining*?

12 What challenge faced Kirk Douglas's military lawyer in *Paths of Glory*?

★ Who discuss 'snails' and 'oysters' in an innuendo-laden scene now restored to *Spartacus*?

TB Who straddled a nuclear bomb as it sailed down to oblivion, a-whoopin' and a-hollerin'?

[86]

THE GANGSTER MOVIE

(S) If you found your favourite horse's head in bed with you, who might it be a present from?

1 Which Hollywood studio was synonymous with gangster movies in the thirties?

2 What did James Cagney assault Jean Harlow with in *The Public Enemy*?

3 What kind of law enforcement officer was Elliott Ness in the various incarnations of *The Untouchables*?

4 Where did Gabriel Byrne pretend to execute John Turturro?

5 And who Tommy-gunned his would-be assassins to the strains of 'Danny Boy' in the same film?

6 Who were considered the star triumvirate of the Warners gangster cycle?

7 Who played *Scarface* in 1932, and 1983?

8 Who were Warren Beatty's leading ladies in *Bonnie and Clyde* and *Dick Tracey*?

9 Why did James Cagney pretend to be a coward when he went to the Chair in *Angels with Dirty Faces*?

10 Paul Muni, Edward G. Robinson, Robert De Niro and Rod Steiger have all portrayed whom on screen?

11 Was Robert De Niro's hoodlum in *Once Upon a Time in America* Irish, Jewish or Sicilian?

12 Who were the guys who killed a boy bartender, pistol-whipped a loutish neighbour, torched night-clubs and pulled off a Lufthansa heist?

★ Is *Brother Orchid* the story of (a) a mobster who becomes a monk to escape his past, (b) a gangster's moll who offers to turn her gay brother straight, or (c) of mobster Texas Guinan and her partner, Larry Fay?

TB 'Made it, ma – top of the world!' The actor and the film?

[87]

LAWRENCE OF ARABIA

(S) 'Ooh, it damn well 'urts!' What was the secret of holding the burning match?

1 How did General Murray describe the Arabian theatre of the First World War in relation to the fighting against the Turks, and in Europe?

2 What was the point of attacking Aqaba from the Nefud Desert?

3 Who bristled when Lawrence encouraged Prince Feisal to use guerrilla tactics, rather than conventional warfare?

4 Who brought the same distinguished hand to *Lawrence of Arabia*'s script as to *A Man for all Seasons*?

5 How did Lawrence's two boys die?

6 Who couldn't have wished for a more scintillating entry into western cinema, than when he emerged from a dusty horizon to claim his own?

7 'No sir, I can't claim to have known him. I once had the honour to shake his hand in Damascus.' What had the old blimp also unknowingly done when Lawrence was in Arab disguise?

8 Why were the British Army reluctant to give the Arab forces artillery?

9 A member of the Harith killed one of the Howitat. If he went unpunished, the Howitat would be aggrieved. If they retaliated, a blood feud would begin. How was the dilemma resolved?

10 Where did Lawrence's underlying desire for adulation get the better of him, and he posed for a photograph?

11 Lawrence: 'I killed two people. One was yesterday. He was just a boy and I led him into quicksand. The other was ...well ... before Damascus. I had to execute him with my pistol and there was something about it I didn't like.'
Allenby: 'That's to be expected.'
Lawrence: 'No, something else.'
Allenby: 'Well, then let it be a lesson.'
Lawrence: 'No ... something else.'
Allenby: 'What then?'
What indeed?

12 How did Lawrence eventually die?

★ What was the one way of cajoling Auda Abu Tayi (Anthony Quinn) to ride on Aqaba that wouldn't offend his sense of independence?

TB Who said, 'You know, I can't make out whether you're bloody bad-mannered, or just half-witted'?

[88]

JAMES STEWART

(5) Who or what is *Harvey*?

1 'Either I'm dead right or I'm crazy!' The youthful desperation of who going where?

2 With whom did reporter Mike Connor get drunk and go skinny-dipping in *The Philadelphia Story*?

3 And with whom did a drunk Stewart in real life try to dig his way under a fence into Greta Garbo's home?

4 During the War, did Stewart command a Marine battalion, a minesweeper, a fighter squadron or a bomber squadron?

5 What is unusual about the man George Bailey saves from drowning in *It's a Wonderful Life*?

6 And what spoils George's and Mary's clothes at the dance?

7 How does Stewart stave off Raymond Burr's murderous advance in *Rear Window*?

8 What was the name of Jeff Chandler's Apache chief in *Broken Arrow*?

9 How does Dave Waggoman (Alex Nicol) cripple Will Lockhart (Stewart) in *The Man from Laramie*?

10 When Stewart expressed doubt about acting being a decent profession, who asked him if he thought it more decent to drop bombs on people?

11 In *Shenandoah*, when and where does Stewart's son, Boy (who had been captured by Union soldiers), reappear?

12 How does Ben Gazzara's soldier reward Stewart's defence lawyer, who saved him from a murder charge in *Anatomy of a Murder*?

★ What real crime inspired the macabre premise of *Rope*?

TB What was Stewart's home state?

[89]
CLARK GABLE

(S) Which character said, 'I'm very drunk, and I intend on getting still drunker before this evening's over'?

1 What great event is depicted in *San Francisco*?

2 Why does Peter Warne first help Ellie Andrews in *It Happened One Night*?

3 In *Mutiny on the Bounty*, did Gable play Captain Bligh, Fletcher Christian or Captain Nelson?

4 Who was Big John McMasters' partner in the oil business in *Boom Town*?

5 Who did Gable say 'damn near gave me a heart attack', and on which film?

6 Which John Ford film was tagged as 'Flaming love found in the savage heart of the jungle!'?

7 How much was Gable paid for *Gone with the Wind*: $12,000, $120,000 or $1.2 million?

8 David O. Selznick said, 'Oh, Gable has enemies all right, but ...' What?

9 Who was Gable's third wife?

10 'All right. If that makes you feel any better', says Gable, after being slapped by Mary Astor. The film?

11 Who was Gable's co-star in *Dance, Fools, Dance*?

12 'Hello, honeybun. Miss me?'
'No, I can always go to the zoo when you're away.'
'Oh, I've got rivals, huh?'
Gable and Eve Arden in which film?

★ Which mogul told Gable's mentor, Lionel Barrymore, 'Look at those big, batlike ears! Forget it, Lionel!'?

TB Which comic called him, 'The best ears of our lives'?

[90]
QUENTIN TARANTINO

(**S**) What do they call a Quarter Pounder in France?

1 If Mr Blonde is torturing a cop, what's on the radio?

2 How exactly do we see Mr Blonde cut off the cop's ear?

3 From whose novel is *Jackie Brown* adapted?

4 Why did John Travolta leave his gun lying around for Bruce Willis to pick up and kill him with?

5 Who doesn't tip unless he feels the service genuinely merits it?

6 What was Tarantino's contribution to *True Romance*?

7 Which star of 70s 'blaxploitation' movies played Jackie Brown?

8 An undercover cop in *Reservoir Dogs* and a robber who picks the wrong restaurant to rob in *Pulp Fiction*. The British actor?

9 Who languished in low-key roles in such as *Jurassic Park* before his towering performance in *Pulp Fiction*?

10 And what's in his briefcase?

11 Name one of the objections raised by the *Reservoir Dogs* gang to their code names.

12 Why is *From Dusk till Dawn* a period of particular danger?

★ Why is Christopher Walken's Sicilian hood offended to the point of shooting Dennis Hopper in *True Romance*?

TB *Taxi Driver* and *Pulp Fiction*. The actor?

[91]

JAMES CAMERON

(S) What was Kate Winslet wearing when Leo DiCaprio sketched her?

1 'Get away from her, you *bitch!*' Who are the warring mother figures, and in which film?

2 Why didn't many of the extras strolling about the *Titanic* have to be paid?

3 What problem does a calm sea present to ships' lookouts searching for icebergs?

4 Why were Ripley and Newt menaced by alien larvae in the medical wing?

5 Which jeopardy wasn't presented in *The Abyss*: a hurricane, nuclear warheads, a killer epidemic, a pressure-crazy Navy Seal, mysterious aliens, or, er, an abyss?

6 The first *Terminator* seemed to have been incinerated in a petrol-tanker fire. What was the equivalent event in *T2: Judgement Day*?

7 How in *T2* did Arnie demonstrate to the cyberscientist that he was one of his creations?

8 Which actor links *The Terminator*, *Aliens* and *The Abyss*?

9 How does the *Titanic*'s Captain Smith drown?

10 How did Ripley get the alien queen to call off her consorts?

11 Which film's tally of eleven Oscars did *Titanic* equal?

12 In *The Abyss*, what kind of breathing did Ed Harris have to relearn?

★ How many wrong Sarah Connors did the original Terminator kill?

TB How did Sarah finally kill the original Terminator?

[92]
INGRID BERGMAN

(S) With whom does Bergman have an intense fling in *Notorious*?

1 What was Bergman's US debut, a remake of a Swedish romance between a piano teacher and a married man?

2 Which Israeli Prime Minister did Bergman portray?

3 Which mogul lured her to Hollywood?

4 'I would kiss you, but where do the noses go?' The film?

5 What hush-hush substance gave *Notorious* its McGuffin?

6 Bergman's affair with which Italian director seriously harmed her career?

7 The publicity machine touted Bergman as 'Sweden's greatest export since ...'? Ingmar Bergman? Garbo? Volvo?

8 In *Casablanca*, what were Ilse's maiden and married names?

9 Which martyr was Bergman a little old to play?

10 Who wanted to shoot a sequence of a statue cracking apart, with ants crawling over it, and underneath Bergman, covered by ants? For which film?

11 What is Charles Boyer trying to do to Bergman in *Gaslight*?

12 Name two of the three films for which she won Oscars.

★ In *Stromboli*, Bergman has fled to Italy from where? Finland, Poland, Lithuania or Estonia?

TB In which film did Bergman, Ingmar, direct Bergman, Ingrid?

[93]

BRITISH FILM

(S) Zither music. Harry Lime. A Ferris Wheel. Which Carol Reed film?

1   Who formed a comic triumvirate with Moore Marriott and Graham Moffatt in the persona of a slightly crooked incompetent?

2   Whose films, in Britain until 1940, were made according to the philosophy, 'Always make the audience suffer as much as possible'?

3   How did the Lavender Hill Mob disguise their stolen gold?

4   What did Ray Brooks have in 1965 that Michael Crawford wanted to learn?

5   Which Hungarian producer-director, of huge importance to British film in the thirties, oversaw films like *The Thief of Baghdad*, *The Four Feathers* and *Rembrandt*?

6   What would you be seeking if you encountered a catapulted cow, a man-eating rabbit, and the Knights who say 'Ni'?

7   Why was the ending of *The Man in the White Suit* a happy one for the trade unions?

8   Which 1996 film saw a Sean Connery impersonator shoot a dog with an air-rifle?

9   Who directed, and who produced, such films as *The Red Shoes*, *A Matter of Life and Death* and *The Life and Death of Colonel Blimp*?

10 For which studios did Christopher Lee and Peter Cushing make many blood-soaked shoestring epics?

11 Which Laurence Olivier production travelled from the Globe Theatre to France to help raise wartime morale?

12 Who pretended to play music in Miss Lop-sided's house?

★   From which respective countries did the quintessentially English actors Robert Donat, Leslie Howard and Laurence Harvey originate?

TB Who played Rommel, Captain Nero, Brutus and *Odd Man Out*?

[94]
SEAN CONNERY

(S) What is *The Rock*?

1 Before stardom, what did Connery polish for a living?

2 What kind of drivers were Connery, Patrick McGoohan and Stanley Baker?

3 Name three actors who have played Blofeld to Connery's 007

4 At which of Goldfinger's homes did Bond roll in the hay with Pussy Galore (the US state and type of establishment please)

5 Where did Connery compete for Scotland in 1953?

6 Which Umberto Eco adaptation won him a British Academy Award?

7 How did Connery use a dead man to get a living man to talk in *The Untouchables*?

8 If Hitler autographs his notebook, then who's Connery's son?

9 Which weak *Alien* derivative saw Connery as a marshal on a space colony?

10 What was his role in *Dragonheart*?

11 Where did Connery pick up a love of golf?

12 The Bonds of which three actors are sandwiched between Connery's outings in *Goldfinger* and *Diamonds are Forever*?

★ How does Connery link screen roles by Audrey Hepburn and Mary Elizabeth Mastrantonio?

TB Knowing a lot about Sean Connery is hardly a substitute for moral fibre. The film?

[95]

ASIAN CINEMA

(S) Is *Tampopo* a celebration of ninjutsu, noodles, Nikon or the Burma Railway?

1 Whose enthusiasm brought Hong Kong director John Woo to Western prominence?

2 What nickname was given to the Madan studio built in the Calcutta suburb of Tollygunge?

3 Nikkatsu and Shochiku were the largest early production companies in which country?

4 *Tsahal* is an enthralling study of the defence forces of which country?

5 If Gong Li is betrothed to a leprous winemaker, what's growing in the fields?

6 Where is *The Simpsons* mostly animated?

7 Which southern Indian city was by 1980 producing more films than anywhere else in the world?

8 Name the leader who commissioned *Al-Qadissa*, about a seventh-century Iraqi victory over Persia?

9 What was Mira Nair's 1988 hit, a cheerful tale of a young urchin in the big city?

10 Japanese cinephiles flew to Paris in 1976 to see the uncut version of which film?

11 Who is a regular John Woo star: Gong Li, Bert Kwouk, Chow Yun-Fat or Jackie Chan?

12 What war of occupation was depicted in Cai Chusheng and Zheng Junli's *The Spring River Flows East*?

★ In *Kagemusha*, why do the commanders of a fortress get their best sniper to mark with stones his exact shooting position at the battlements?

TB Who played Kato in the US crime show *The Green Hornet*?

[96]
FILM ACTING

(S) Who has played a gay Nazi punk, a cerebral palsy sufferer, an adopted American Indian trapper and a small-time Belfast crook?

1 Who created New York's Actors' Studio, whose alumni have gathered over a hundred Oscar nominations?

2 What name is given to the technique he inherited from Stanislavsky, of using memories of past experiences to make your performance more emotionally truthful?

3 Which fictional character has been portrayed on screen more often than any other?

4 For which 1942 movie were Ronald Reagan and Ann Sheridan the original choice of leads?

5 As Dustin Hoffman staggered in, fresh from getting into character for *Marathon Man*, who (reputedly) said, 'My dear boy, have you ever tried acting?'

6 Whose more filmic acting style made Olivier seem rather mannered in *Sleuth*?

7 Who spent 125 features playing Marion Morrison?

8 Which formidable thespian family included John, Lionel and Ethel?

9 Who is the only actress to have won four Oscars?

10 And who said, 'I stopped believing in Santa Claus when I was six. My mother took me to see him in a department store, and he asked for my autograph'?

11 Who found acting the lead in *The Red Shoes* traumatic, as she was solely a dancer?

12 Who was known as The Man of a Thousand Faces?

★ Who is the only actor to speak in Mel Brooks's *Silent Movie*?

TB When questioned about his statement that 'Actors are cattle', what did Hitchcock change it to?

[97]

DAVID LEAN

(S) Who came from a fat country called Oxfordshire?

1 In which department of film-making (a good education for a director) did Lean start out before Noël Coward gave him his directorial break?

2 What railway network was *The Bridge on the River Kwai* a part of?

3 Who fell in love with a British officer in Ireland during the First World War?

4 Which classic begins with crooked branches and ruffled pools against a gathering storm sky?

5 Who was Pip's mysterious benefactor?

6 And how did Miss Haversham die?

7 Which Conrad novel was Lean planning to adapt when he died?

8 For whose love were Omar Sharif and Rod Steiger rivals in *Doctor Zhivago*?

9 Was Lean's last film (a) *Northwest Passage*, (b) *Passage to Marseilles*, (c) *A Passage to India*, or (d) *Passenger 57*?

10 Who did Alec Guinness and Robert Newton play in *Oliver Twist*?

11 After Rex Harrison's performance in *Blithe Spirit*, who said to him, 'After me you're the best light comedian in the world'?

12 What did Celia Johnson and Trevor Howard have on Stanley Holloway's platform?

★ Which impish fellow director observed that the serious Lean's forehead would crease up like 'all the railway lines from *Brief Encounter*'?

TB The British equivalent of *The Right Stuff*?

[98]
THE COEN BROTHERS

(5) Johnny Caspar wants to bump off Bernie Bernbaum, whom he suspects of revealing his fixed fights, but Leo wants Bernie protected because he's courting his sister, only Tom Reagan thinks she's playing Leo for a sap (not to mention that Tom's bedding her too), so Tom defects from Leo to Caspar (only he's not), who trusts Tom, whereas Eddie Dane is more than suspicious. Meanwhile the Dane is sweet with Mink LaRouey, who's sweet with Bernie Bernbaum ... Bring along your thinking cap for which majestic gangster drama?

1   'You know, for kids!' What?

2   Who's the highbrow Broadway playwright lured to Hollywood to write a wrestling picture?

3   In *Miller's Crossing*, what song is playing on the gramophone when Albert Finney shows he's still an artist with a tommy gun?

4   What is the Coen brothers' home state?

5   Barton Fink, Bernie Bernbaum, Quintana. The actor?

6   How do Holly Hunter's and Nicolas Cage's professions bring them together in *Raising Arizona*?

7   Why is Frances McDormand's Minnesota cop a little slower on her feet than normal in *Fargo*?

8   The sleazy private eye in *Blood Simple*. The sleazy police chief in *Blade Runner*. The actor?

9   Which brother is (nominally, at least) the producer, and which the director?

10 How does Waring Hudsucker depart the Hudsucker boardroom for the last time?

11 Which of the following actors is not a Coen regular: John Goodman, Jeff Bridges, Frances McDormand, Steve Buscemi?

12 What's the predominant European stock of the town of Fargo?

★   Whose story, *The Glass Key*, partly inspired *Miller's Crossing*?

TB How does the moment's silence in memory of Mr Hudsucker's death most directly affect his employees?

[99]

FILM NOIR

(S) Why are Humphrey Bogart, Lauren Bacall and Edward G. Robinson cooped up together in a *Key Largo* hotel?

1 What links John Huston to *The Maltese Falcon* and *Chinatown* respectively?

2 How many times had *The Maltese Falcon* already been filmed when Bogart and Huston took their turn?

3 In which film did Richard Widmark debut memorably as a maniacally laughing psychopath?

4 In *The Big Sleep*, what commodity did Philip Marlowe feel was in shorter supply than guns?

5 A reluctant gumshoe. A *femme fatale* (in more ways than one). A future-noir vision of dark, rain-washed cityscapes. The film?

6 What is *chiaroscuro*?

7 Which Elia Kazan film was based on the unsolved 1924 murder of a priest in Connecticut?

8 Who agreed to murder Barbara Stanwyck's husband for the insurance money?

9 'By gad, sir, you're a fellow worth knowing, a character. No telling what you'll say next, except that it will be something astonishing.' Who's getting Sam Spade to let down his guard?

10 Why did Huston cast the actor who dies after bringing Spade the Falcon?

11 Name the noir spoof where Steve Martin costars with Bogart, Cagney, MacMurray and Stanwyck, among others.

12 'When you're slapped, you're going to take it and like it!' Says who to whom, in *Across the Pacific*?

★ In *M* (one of the dark German films which in part anticipated the noir atmosphere), which body of people help the police to track down Peter Lorre's child-murderer?

TB A cable channel in *Gremlins 2: The New Batch* advertises a new version of *Casablanca* with what two changes?

[100]
THE GODFATHER

(S) Who wrote the novel?

1 'Johnny Fontaine will never get that movie! I don't care how many dago guinea wop greaseball goombahs come out of the woodwork!' What changes Jack Woltz's mind?

2 Is Robert Duvall's adopted son of the family Italian-Irish, Italian-German or Irish-German?

3 How many times, to the nearest ten, is the word 'Mafia' mentioned in *The Godfather*?

4 Who was offered the direction of *The Godfather*, preferring instead to prepare *Once Upon a Time in America*?

5 Who plays Fredo?

6 Was the young Michael toughened up in World War I, World War II, Korea or Vietnam?

7 Does Michael dispose of Fredo in a restaurant, on a lake, in an aeroplane or in an orange orchard?

8 'Don Corleone, I am honoured and grateful that you have invited me to your house on the day of your daughter's wedding.' The character, nervously rehearsing his spiel to Don Vito?

9 Who stood in for Winona Ryder in *The Godfather Part III*, to universal brickbats and accusations of nepotism?

10 Who composed the score?

11 Exactly what Oscar did Francis Ford Coppola win for *The Godfather*?

12 How does Michael's first wife die?

★ That Luca Brasi sleeps with the fishes is announced by the delivery of what?

TB Who isn't related to Francis Ford Coppola: Talia Shire, Richard Conte, Nicolas Cage or Jason Schwartzman?

[101]

BUSTER KEATON

(5) What was Keaton's nickname: Mile Wide Smile, Stone Face, the Tramp or the King of Hollywood?

1 Who was so impressed by the infant Keaton's resilience (as a vaudeville performer with his parents) that he named him Buster?

2 Which old friend, now a star comic himself, gave Keaton his first break in movies?

3 Which component of *The Electric House* broke his ankle?

4 In *Our Hospitality*, why does Keaton do everything possible to avoid leaving the Canfield household?

5 Which studio did Joseph Schenk buy, renaming it the Keaton studio?

6 What was unique about the stunt in *College* where Keaton pole-vaults through the girl's window?

7 Which film was based on the true story of Unionist Captain Anderson's seizure of a Confederate train?

8 How is *The General* saved from the blast of the flatcar cannon?

9 True or false: (in perhaps the costliest silent gag of them all) *The General* crashes to oblivion through a burning, collapsing bridge.

10 With whom does Keaton struggle to give a violin and piano recital in *Limelight*?

11 Which film found Keaton and Kathryn McGuire adrift on a deserted transatlantic liner?

12 One questionnaire for applicants to the Keaton studio consisted of two questions: 1. Can you act? 2. Can you play baseball? What was the pass mark?

★ How did Keaton break his neck (without even realising it) during *Sherlock Jr*?

TB Of which D. W. Griffith movie was *The Three Ages* a spoof?

[102]

JODIE FOSTER

(S) What is Foster listening for at the beginning of *Contact*?

1 Foster's first screen break, as a three-year-old, was having her knickers pulled down by a dog, to advertise (a) Andrex toilet tissue, (b) Pet Behave aerosols, or (c) Coppertan sun tan lotion?

2 For which studio did the young Foster make *Napoleon and Samantha*, *Freaky Friday* and *Candleshoe*?

3 Before which role was the twelve-year-old Foster required to undergo psychological tests to see if her morals would bear up during filming?

4 What did John Hinckley Jr decide was the best way to woo Foster?

5 What flavour of accent did Hannibal Lecter know Clarice Starling was trying to conceal?

6 Who had been the firm favourite for the Best Actress Oscar when Foster scooped it for *The Silence of the Lambs*?

7 In what crime were *The Accused*, the onlookers in a bar, complicit?

8 In which film did Martin Scor..sese direct Foster prior to *Taxi Driver*?

9 Splurge guns, pedal cars, and an all-child cast unequal to the task of acting against Foster. The Alan Parker film?

10 In *Contact*, space travel machines are built to the alien specifications in America and which other country?

11 In which film did the once-precocious Foster direct herself as the mother of a young prodigy?

12 Who starred opposite Foster in *Sommersby*, and whose original French role was he reprising?

★ From which university did Foster graduate with Honours?

TB Who had been first choice for the role of Clarice Starling?

[103]

SHAKESPEARE
IN THE MOVIES

(S) Who played *Romeo and Juliet* in Baz Luhrmann's version, which substituted Verona Beach for Verona?

1 Which D. W. Griffith adaptation was billed as having 'additional dialogue by Sam Taylor'?

2 What kind of society did Ian McKellen relocate *Richard III* to?

3 In *Shakespeare in Love*, what ritual does Will go through before sitting down to write?

4 What is Will's first stab at *Romeo and Juliet* going to be called?

5 What connects the Will of *Shakespeare in Love* to 1995's Tony Award winning *Hamlet* on Broadway ?

6 In 1956's *Forbidden Planet*, a loose reworking of *The Tempest*, who or what represents Ariel?

7 Before *Shakespeare in Love*, Tom Stoppard wrote a play about two minor characters from *Hamlet*. The title?

8 What do *Romeo and Juliet*'s Montague and Capulet clans become in Leonard Bernstein's *West Side Story*?

9 What is the most obvious change made to Lear's daughters in Akira Kurosawa's version, *Ran*?

10 In *Shakespeare in Love*, for what outrage does Tilney try to have the Rose Theatre closed?

11 As well as suffering from writer's block, in whose playwrighting shadow does Will feel himself to be?

12 Who were Laurence Olivier and Kenneth Branagh when they fought on St Crispin's Day?

★ Before his death, *Yellow Submarine* director George Dunning tantalisingly partly finished an animated version of which play?

TB 'Well, that will have them rolling in the aisles.' Hensloe's response to which bit of Will's new play?

[104]
LEONARDO DICAPRIO

(S) Is *Romeo and Juliet*'s first meeting centred around a fish tank, a terrapin tank or a septic tank?

1 Why was DiCaprio given the name Leonardo?

2 Was his television debut in an episode of *Cheers*, *Lassie* or *Remington Steele*?

3 Who plays DiCaprio's brutal stepfather in *This Boy's Life*?

4 In which country did *Titanic* premiere (and DiCaprio receive the full blast of Leomania)?

5 Who play the Four Musketeers to DiCaprio's *The Man in the Iron Mask*?

6 Which was the first feature to bill DiCaprio's name above the title?

7 If DiCaprio's the retarded Arnie, then who's Gilbert?

8 Which rapper co-starred in *The Basketball Diaries*?

9 Did *Titanic* stay at number one in the US box office for fifteen, twenty or twenty-five consecutive weeks?

10 DiCaprio plumped for the role of Jack Dawson in *Titanic* over that of Dirk Diggler in which other movie?

11 What was tragic about River Phoenix wanting the lead role in *The Basketball Diaries*?

12 Before *Romeo and Juliet*, what kind of dancing had director Baz Luhrmann been interested in?

★ Which poet did DiCaprio play in *Total Eclipse*?

TB Kenneth Branagh, Winona Ryder, Joe Mantegna and DiCaprio. The Woody Allen excursion?

[105]

FADE OUT

(S) Which computer-animated feature ends with 'out-takes', as if the 'performers' were real actors?

Which films end with these scenes?

1 A man in a trenchcoat and a French policeman walk off across an airport tarmac.

2 An old man is surprised to find that the lift he thought was going down is actually going up.

3 A man walks along the street, his 'crippled' arm and leg straighten, and he escapes the gaze of the cop he hoodwinked.

4 Escaping the hangman's noose, a man and woman swim off across a lake to freedom.

5 A British Army officer, being driven in a staff car, gazes at a passing motorcycle dispatch rider.

And which films' last lines are these?

6 'It was beauty killed the beast.'

7 'O'Lan, you are the earth.'

8 'Now for Australia and a crack at those Japs!'

9 'I think we oughta leave now.'
   'That's probably a good idea.'

10 'I guess Rosebud is just a piece in a jigsaw puzzle. A missing piece.'

11 Whose last performance was in *The Shooting Party*?

12 And which director's last film was *Eyes Wide Shut*?

★ Which European director, on leaving Hollywood, said, 'Goodbye, Mr Zanuck: it certainly has been a pleasure working at 16th Century Fox'?

TB And in which film does Tim Robbins say, 'Can we talk about something other than Hollywood for a change? We're educated people'?

ANSWERS

[1]
FOUNDING FATHERS

(5) Auguste Lumière

1 (b)

2 Each thread was attached to a still camera at the side. If, for example, a horse galloped down the track, it would trigger a series of photos of its progress

3 Cinématographe, coined by the Lumière brothers

4 1895

5 *Arrival of a Train at the Station* (the train comes almost straight at the camera)

6 Magic Lantern shows

7 A shot where the camera swivels left or right, from the Lumière term 'panorama'

8 The workings of the cinématographe

9 Kodak

10 Teddy Roosevelt

11 They couldn't be filmed often enough

12 The Edison device was far bulkier, and almost immobile

★ Bioscope (bioskop)

TB Georges Méliès

[2]
CHARLIE CHAPLIN

(S) Mussolini (Napaloni)

1   Lambeth
2   A boot
3   As a giant chicken
4   Jackie Coogan
5   Fred Karno
6   Keystone Studios, and the Keystone Cops
7   The House Un-American Activities Committee
8   Claire Bloom
9   Mahatma Gandhi
10 Singing in gibberish Italian
11 By breaking windows for him to fix
12 It got spiked with alcohol
★   *Monsieur Verdoux*
TB His daughter Geraldine Chaplin starred

[3]
DIRECTING

(S) Alfred Hitchcock

1 *Vice-versa*

2 Erich von Stroheim

3 They called their helicopters away to fight rebels

4 Clint Eastwood (respectively *White Hunter, Black Heart*, John Huston and Humphrey Bogart)

5 Orson Welles

6 In outline on a neon sign

7 Michael Curtiz

8 John Boorman (*Deliverance, The Emerald Forest* and *Hope and Glory*)

9 Stanley Kubrick (*Eyes Wide Shut*)

10 The arrangement of everything you can see within the film frame (originally a theatrical term, meaning 'placing on stage')

11 The cut from medieval falcon to Spitfire

12 The Aboriginal Australian flag

★ That a major director is able to stamp their own distinctive artistic imprint on all their films (as opposed to the view that this is impossible in such a collaborative art-form)

TB Ridley Scott (*Alien*)

[4]
ORSON WELLES

(5) The sledge Citizen Kane played with as a child
1 William Randolph Hearst
2 Post-war Vienna
3 The Mercury Theatre Company
4 *Heart of Darkness* (*Apocalypse Now*)
5 *Touch of Evil*
6 *The Magnificent Ambersons*
7 *War of the Worlds*
8 (a) [(b) was *Touch of Evil*, (c) *Black Magic*]
9 *The Trial*, by Franz Kafka
10 *The Lady from Shanghai*
11 Cardinal Wolsey (*A Man for All Seasons*)
12 RKO

★ *Providence*

TB Herman J. Mankiewicz

[5]
GERMAN CINEMA

(S) *Metropolis*

1 *Sunrise*

2 *The Boat (Das Boot)*

3 (b) [(a) was *Triumph of the Will*, (c) *Aguirre, Wrath of God*]

4 *The Tin Drum*

5 *Nosferatu*

6 UFA (Universum Film Aktien Gesellschaft)

7 Joseph von Sternberg

8 Marlene Dietrich

9 Because that was the nearest the locals could get to pronouncing 'Fitzgerald'

10 Eight hours

11 Leni Riefenstahl

12 Rainer Werner Fassbinder

★ Avant-garde animation

TB *Heimat* (which means 'home')

[6]
KATHARINE HEPBURN

(5) A leopard

1 ' … What we were put into this world to rise above.'

2 Cary Grant and James Stewart

3 Spencer Tracy

4 Box office poison

5 From: *Morning Glory*, *Guess Who's Coming to Dinner*, *The Lion in Winter* and *On Golden Pond*

6 By attaching makeshift torpedoes to the bows of the *African Queen*, and ramming it

7 They are opposing lawyers

8 Eleanor of Aquitaine

9 Henry and Jane Fonda

10 The gamut of emotions from A to B

11 *Long Day's Journey into Night*

12 Because she intends to marry a black man (Sidney Poitier)

★ 'You could throw a hat at her, and wherever it hit, it would stick.'

TB John Barrymore

[7]
FILM AND POLITICS

(S) The Watergate break-in
1 Bob Woodward and Carl Bernstein
2 'Deep Throat' (Hal Holbrook)
3 The Spanish Civil War
4 Alan Clarke
5 Tim Roth
6 *The Green Berets*
7 Jimmy Hoffa
8 Sterling Hayden
9 He was an IRA man shot in a hold-up
10 Jodie Foster
11 Tim Robbins
12 Alan Pakula

★ Minister for War

TB Anthony Hopkins

[8]
2001: A SPACE ODYSSEY

(S) (Strauss's) *The Blue Danube*

1   Stanley Kubrick
2   A mysterious monolith
3   He learns to use a bone as a club
4   *The Sentinel*
5   To Jupiter
6   The HAL 9000 computer
7   He had read their lips
8   *In Space, No-one Can Hear You Scream*
9   HAL murdered them by turning off their life-support systems
10   Douglas Trumbull
11   *Daisy, Daisy*
12   Advance each letter one place in the alphabet

★   Heuristically programmed ALgorithmic computer

TB   David Bowie (as Ziggy Stardust, in *Space Oddity*)

[9]
HUMPHREY BOGART

(5) Rick, in *Casablanca* (it was 'Play it, Sam. Play it, for old times' sake')

1 *The Maltese Falcon*

2 *The Roaring Twenties*

3 It came from an injury he received on board ship when he was in the Navy

4 Caspar Gutman (played by Sydney Greenstreet)

5 *The Petrified Forest*

6 *The Treasure of the Sierra Madre*

7 Her $200

8 *The Big Sleep*

9 A paper of transit, that would allow the holder passage ultimately to America

10 On *Key Largo*

11 Captain Queeg (*The Caine Mutiny*)

12 Peter Lorre

★ Conrad Veidt

TB Lauren Bacall

[10]
FRENCH CINEMA

(5) *Nikita*

1 *Les Enfants du Paradis*

2 Jean-Louis Barrault

3 *Rififi*

4 Her husband had faked his own death, and was pretending to be a white-eyed ghost to frighten her to death

5 René Clair

6 The New Wave (La Nouvelle Vague)

7 Erich von Stroheim

8 *La Règle du Jeu*

9 Jean Cocteau

10 They were carrying consignments of nitro-glycerine

11 *Cyrano de Bergerac*

12 Jacques Tati

★ *Last Year at Marienbad*

TB Le Boulevard du Crime

[11]
COMEDY

(5) The Three Stooges

1 One, Cato would politely answer the phone, and two, Clouseau would beat him up anyway

2 Hitchcock

3 *The Life of Brian*

4 Zeppo and Gummo

5 Bob Hope

6 Tom and Jerry

7 To lift their kilts at the enemy

8 *There's Something About Mary*

9 *Airplane!*

10 David Naughton and Griffin Dunne (*An American Werewolf in London*)

11 'Nobody's perfect!'

12 Elliott Ness (*The Untouchables*)

★ Audrey Hepburn

TB Spinal Tap (*This is Spinal Tap!*)

[12]
STEVEN SPIELBERG

(S) Because Spielberg thought Smith was too common

1 The shape of Devil's Chimney, which his UFO encounter had left in his subconscious

2 Velociraptors

3 *Duel*

4 A Great White Shark (as in *Jaws*)

5 Richard Dreyfus and Robert Shaw

6 With *Schindler's List*

7 *E.T.*

8 *1941*

9 *The Color Purple*

10 *Empire of the Sun*

11 *Back to the Future*

12 Jeff Goldblum

★ *Badlands*

TB False (he was 16, *Firelight* cost $300, and it was screened at only [!] one theatre)

[13]
ANIMATORS

⑤ Claymation
1 Gertie the Dinosaur
2 Tex Avery
3 Jan Svankmajer
4 Roger Rabbit (*Who Framed Roger Rabbit*)
5 *The Nightmare Before Christmas*
6 Norman McLaren
7 *Creature Comforts*
8 The National Film Board of Canada
9 Walt Disney
10 *Ballet Mécanique*
11 The Brothers Quay
12 A *Yellow Submarine*
★ Ub Iwerks

TB In Peter Gabriel's *Sledgehammer* video

[14]
THE GREAT WAR

(S) German

1 *Sergeant York*

2 Gary Cooper

3 Camels, and ships sailing eerily down the Suez Canal

4 James Whale

5 Christ

6 *Oh! What a Lovely War*

7 *Gallipoli*

8 *Paths of Glory*

9 The gentlemanly officer class, and the chivalrous way of waging war

10 Reaching out towards a butterfly

11 Air combat (*Wings*)

12 *The Road Back*

★ Adolphe Menjou

TB General Allenby

[15]
SCHINDLER'S LIST

(S) Of a Jewish Krakow

 1 Thomas Keneally
 2 'The presentation'
 3 Ralph Fiennes
 4 The Survivors of the Shoah Visual History Foundation
 5 Can actually be fired
 6 'Who are you? Moses?'
 7 Plaszow
 8 'The world entire'
 9 Shoots a young boy dead from his quarters with his rifle
10 John Williams
11 33 years (*The Apartment*)
12 Roberto Benigni's *Life is Beautiful* (*La Vita è Bella*)

 ★ He was hanged by Poles in Krakow

TB Seven

[16]
ITALIAN CINEMA

(S) *Bicycle Thieves* (US *Bicycle Thief*)

1   Without it, he couldn't get work

2   Neo-realist

3   Dirk Bogarde

4   The *Miracle in Milan*

5   Federico Fellini

6   *L'Avventura*

7   Giuseppe de Lampedusa

8   Bergman married director Roberto Rossellini

9   Marcello Mastroianni

10 A huge enlargement of a photo, made by a photographer (David Hemmings) who thinks it contains evidence of a murder

11 The Cinecitta Studios

12 *Eight and a Half*

★   *The Battle of Algiers*

TB *Cinema Paradiso*

[17]
THE HOLLYWOOD MOGULS

(5) J. Arthur Rank

 1 Funerals
 2 Louis B Mayer
 3 Harry Cohn
 4 'It can't say yes.'
 5 Paramount
 6 Columbia
 7 Sam Goldwyn
 8 Irving Thalberg
 9 The degree of nepotism in Hollywood
10 Because it had so many Cohns
11 A submarine
12 *Rebecca*

 ★ Darryl Zanuck

TB Minsk

[18]
THE ADVENT OF SOUND

(5) *The Jazz Singer*

1   *The Lights of New York*

2   An agreement to commonly adopt the most promising sound system (a Western Electric process) to avoid a Babel of incompatible systems

3   RKO

4   Thomas Edison

5   Sarcastically, because, as Jesse Lasky described, 'the poor cameraman emerged from [the booth's] tight confines after a long take, parboiled and gasping for breath.'

6   Because the technique of mixing music or other effects onto the soundtrack hadn't yet been devised – if you wanted music in the scene, the music had to be played then and there

7   *Blackmail*

8   Alan Crosland

9   A padded covering to muffle the whirring of the camera

10   *Wings*

11   Tallulah Bankhead

12   Germany

★   Eisenstein

TB   Neil Diamond

[19]
ALFRED HITCHCOCK

(5) The Bates Motel (*Psycho*)

1 He had a partial recollection of a murder on a ski slope
2 *Rebecca*
3 James Stewart (*Rear Window*)
4 *Rope*
5 On the Scottish moors, in *The Thirty-Nine Steps*
6 Tippi Hedren
7 Salvador Dali
8 Chocolate sauce
9 Andrew Sarris
10 That each murder the person of most trouble to the other
11 *Vertigo*
12 Cary Grant

★ Leo G. Carroll

TB Carole Lombard

[20]

SOVIET AND RUSSIAN CINEMA

⑤ Lenin

1 Andrei Tarkovsky

2 *Mr West* (directed by Lev Kuleshov)

3 Sergei Eisenstein

4 Constructivism

5 *October* (Eisenstein)

6 *Chapayev* (Sergei and Georgy Vasiliev)

7 Vsevolod Pudovkin

8 The priest

9 *Andrei Rublev*

10 Dziga Vertov

11 *Little Vera*

12 Inside a giant hammer-and-sickle sign

★ Soyuzkino

TB Alexander Dovzhenko

[21]

THE WESTERN

(5) *The Magnificent Seven*

1   Gary Cooper

2   *Shane*

3   Gene Hackman's Sheriff in *Unforgiven*

4   *The Paleface*

5   *Little Big Man* and *The Outlaw Josey Wales*

6   John Ford

7   Lee Marvin

8   Cecil B. De Mille

9   *The Great Train Robbery*

10 *A Fistful of Dollars* and *A Fistful of Dynamite*

11 James Stewart

12 *Blazing Saddles*

★   *Boom Town*

TB False – it was Clint Westwood

[22]
THE FILM IMAGE

(S) *Saving Private Ryan*

1 David Lean (for *Lawrence of Arabia*)

2 The aperture of the camera lens (how much light it lets in)

3 A widescreen effect produced by putting three frames side by side

4 *Kwaidan*

5 *Trainspotting*

6 An optical effect where the shot becomes a diminishing circular disc against black, until it vanishes altogether

7 Nicolas Roeg

8 Gregg Toland

9 The key light

10 In *Fantasia*

11 To segue into a sequence of sepia-tinted snapshots (or to indicate a lifestyle now in the past)

12 *2001: A Space Odyssey*

★ Extreme depth of field photography

TB *Blade Runner*

[23]

MARTIN SCORSESE

Ⓢ A *Taxi Driver*

1 *Goodfellas*

2 Jerry Lewis

3 *After Hours*

4 *Raging Bull*

5 He ballooned in weight and became a night-club owner

6 The Band; *The Last Waltz*

7 Joe Pesci

8 That of Cody the psychopath in *Cape Fear*

9 He was a 'made man', a senior council member, and had to be avenged

10 *The Last Temptation of Christ*

11 *The Age of Innocence*

12 *Alice Doesn't Live Here Anymore*

★ He made a quick-draw device which fitted his arm and slid a gun into his hand

TB De Niro and Pesci

[24]
DREAMS AND FANTASIES

(5) Freddy Kreuger

1   In *The Company of Wolves*

2   Willy Wonka (in *Willy Wonka and the Chocolate Factory*)

3   *The Wizard of Oz*

4   Jan Svankmajer

5   *Un Chien Andalou*

6   Michael Powell

7   *The Book of Revelation*

8   Basil Radford and Naunton Wayne

9   He was after the fortune stuffed into her doll; *The Night of the Hunter*

10 A quarter (one of the four)

11 *Orphée*

12 *Monty Python and the Holy Grail*

★   *Street of Crocodiles*

TB Bugs

[25]
TITANIC

(5) He won it at poker

1 Rose DeWitt Bukater (now Rose Calvert)
2 Cal Hockley
3 The White Star Line
4 $200 million
5 'I see you.'
6 They are for playing the same character (Rose Bukater/Calvert)
7 Paramount and Twentieth Century Fox
8 Three-quarters actual size
9 The *Carpathia*
10 Philadelphia
11 He was shot by a crewman
12 Southampton

★ 360

TB John Jacob Astor

[26]
SPECIAL EFFECTS

(S) Because there is little blue in human flesh tones (this prevents people from shimmering or disappearing)

1 Onto his scene he superimposed a shot of his head as he was pulled towards the camera on a trolley. This gave the impression that his head was being inflated

2 Stop-motion animation

3 *Who Framed Roger Rabbit*

4 A painting of a scene which has areas left blank – footage of the painting is combined with live action footage in these areas to provide a convincing setting for the action

5 *The Thief of Bagdad*

6 Ray Harryhausen

7 Extra noises added to a sound, e.g. bells, horns or whistles to an explosion, to make it more interesting

8 *Nosferatu*

9 *2001: A Space Odyssey*

10 Pixillation

11 *Man with a Movie Camera*

12 *Jurassic Park*

★ By filming at more than the usual 24 frames per second (25 for video). This effect reverses itself on projection, where the model will seem heavy and ponderous

TB *Terminator 2: Judgement Day*

[27]

AKIRA KUROSAWA

⑤ *The Magnificent Seven* (!)
1   *Hidden Fortress*
2   By using extreme telephoto lenses
3   The murder of a lord and the rape of his lady
4   It's based on *Macbeth*
5   *Bicycle Thieves*
6   George Lucas and Francis Ford Coppola
7   We never find out
8   Toshiro Mifune
9   *Ikiru* (*Living*)
10 Slow motion
11 Toshiro Mifune
12 As Japan's most 'western' director
★   Takashi Shimura
TB The daughters were changed to sons

[28]

STAR WARS

(S) False – it was long ago

1   Two (it was a binary star system)

2   He was working there as a carpenter

3   Grand Moff Tarkin

4   Those of the cantina creature costumes, because no one had remembered to put air vents in them

5   Tunisia

6   The Jawas

7   The Jedi Knights

8   *THX 1138*

9   Anthony Daniels, to make a body cast for C3PO's costume

10 The *Millennium Falcon*

11 It was taped flat to her chest

12 Mark Hamill

★   The robot in Fritz Lang's *Metropolis*

TB After Reel 2, Dialogue 2 (R2, D2) of footage

[29]
CINEMA IN WORLD WAR II

⑤ *Objective, Burma!*

1 *The Battle of San Pietro*

2 The US authorities ordered it to be cut out

3 By submarine

4 *Jew Süss*

5 Erich von Stroheim

6 *In Which We Serve*

7 *Why We Fight*

8 Joseph Goebbels

9 Because the Cathedral's windows had been removed due to the air raids

10 *The Battle of Midway*

11 The Merchant Navy

12 El Alamein

★ *A Diary for Timothy*

TB Britain

[30]
D. W. GRIFFITH

(S) *The Birth of a Nation*
1   Cecil B. De Mille
2   'Roaring Jake' (Jacob Griffith)
3   Lillian Gish
4   The Ku Klux Klan
5   Thomas H Ince or Mack Sennett
6   The First World War
7   Three and a half hours
8   *Love the Stranger in Thy Midst*
9   *The Clansman*
10 'Lightning'
11 St Bartholomew's Day
12 *Abraham Lincoln*
★   The Stonemans or the Camerons

TB Stanley Kubrick

[31]
WORLD CLASSICS

(5) Omar Sharif
 1 Gong Li
 2 Ingmar Bergman
 3 India
 4 Carl Dreyer
 5 Israel
 6 *Andrei Rublev*
 7 Switzerland
 8 Toshiro Mifune
 9 Leopoldo Torre-Nilsson
 10 Pedro Almodóvar
 11 Buried alive in a coffin
 12 *Kagemusha*
 ★ A dye factory
 TB India

[32]
TIM BURTON

(S) *Batman*

1 Disney

2 Vincent Price (*Vincent*)

3 *Beetlejuice*

4 Alan Arkin

5 Danny Elfman

6 *Ed Wood*

7 It might conceal an oversized Martian brain

8 Halloween Town (in *A Nightmare Before Christmas*)

9 The Easter Bunny (*A Nightmare Before Christmas* again)

10 Johnny Depp and Winona Ryder (who were embarking on a real-life romance)

11 *Pee-Wee Herman*

12 Sheep-shearing

★ Armature puppet animation

TB A dog

[33]

ALEC GUINNESS

(5) Fagin

1 *The Bridge on the River Kwai*

2 In the Eiffel Tower

3 Prince Feisal

4 Street lighting

5 A *Spy*

6 *Kind Hearts and Coronets*

7 He was blown up in his own darkroom

8 Ben (Obi-Wan) Kenobi

9 A Highland Regiment

10 He had a wife in two ports

11 He left behind a diary detailing his crimes

12 Yoda (*The Empire Strikes Back*)

★ Herbert Pocket (*Great Expectations*)

TB A railway signal came down on his head

[34]
DARK FUTURES

(S) So that she would never have the son who one day would lead the fight against its kind

1   *THX 1138*

2   Everyone was executed when they reached that age

3   The *Dark Star*

4   Gotham City (*Batman*)

5   *Alien*

6   *Brazil*

7   A *Predator*

8   (c)

9   Ridley Scott (*Blade Runner*)

10   She was kitted up in a power loader

11   *Robocop*

12   The T1000 Terminator

★   *Tetsuo: The Iron Man*

TB   Because Stanley Kubrick banned the screening and distribution of his own *A Clockwork Orange*

[35]
THE MUSICAL

(5) *Romeo and Juliet*

1 New York

2 In *The Rocky Horror Picture Show*

3 The sound era

4 Sidney Poitier

5 *My Favourite Things* (*The Sound of Music*)

6 Irving Berlin

7 Fred Astaire and Ginger Rogers in *Top Hat*

8 Fagin's band of pickpockets (*Oliver!*)

9 The Jets (white) and the Sharks (Puerto Rican)

10 They're sailors with a 24-hour pass

11 *Oklahoma!*

12 *High Society*

★ *A Funny Thing Happened on the Way to the Forum*

TB *Gold Diggers* (there were others, but '33–'37 was the continuous run)

[36]
AUSTRALIAN CINEMA

(S) *The Piano*

 1 *Picnic at Hanging Rock*
 2 Mel Gibson (*Attack Force Z*, *Gallipoli*, the *Mad Max* movies and *Braveheart* respectively)
 3 A turn of the century half-caste, rejected by both communities, finally killed a number of whites with an axe
 4 By human hands (she by his harpoon, he by a lorry driver)
 5 The order not to go over the top (or they would be, and did get, cut to pieces by Turkish troops)
 6 *A Boy and His Dog*
 7 (b) [(a) was *The Club*, and (c) *Tim*]
 8 Peter Weir (*Witness*)
 9 Michael Hutchence (of INXS)
10 Nicole Kidman (*Bangkok Hilton*)
11 Fred Schepisi
12 A light aeroplane that crashed in remote highlands in the thirties
 ★ Charles Chauvel

TB *Mad Max*

[37]
POWELL
AND PRESSBURGER

(**5**) Heaven (in *A Matter of Life and Death*)

1 The Glue Man, who put glue in their hair

2 He stabbed them with his camera tripod as he filmed them

3 Hungarian

4 There were no gentlemanly rules to war any more, and Britain would have to fight as dirty as the Nazis to win

5 He says he can't believe he ever fitted into such a small thing, and challenges him to prove it

6 Moira Shearer

7 An overpowering perfume

8 Jean Simmons

9 Wendy Hiller (Joan Webster, in *I Know Where I'm Going*)

10 The Archers

11 Hoffmann (in *The Tales of Hoffmann*)

12 He sabotaged a U-Boat he had built for them so that it would sink, and had to be on board during its maiden voyage so as not to cause suspicion

★ From: Ludwig Berger, Tim Whelan, Zoltan Korda, William Cameron Menzies or Alexander Korda

TB The *Graf Spee*

[38]

TRAINSPOTTING

(S) Edinburgh

1 People

2 Valium

3 Sean Connery

4 The Worst Toilet in Scotland

5 A *Lust for Life*

6 Ziggy Pop

7 Archie Gemmell scored for Scotland against Holland

8 Her school uniform – she's only 15

9 His neglected kitten's faeces give him toxoplasmosis

10 Sick Boy's dead baby

11 He makes off with the takings from the drug deal

12 Renton (feeling sorry for him) leaves Spud his cut in a locker

★ *Cracker*

TB Orange

[39]
ROCK 'N' ROLL

(**5**) The Beatles (in *Yellow Submarine*)

1 The Band

2 David Bowie

3 *The Blues Brothers*

4 Elvis Presley

5 Spinal Tap (in *This is Spinal Tap*)

6 Wayne (in *Wayne's World*)

7 He's very clean

8 Elton John

9 The prop-makers misread feet for inches on their scruffy sketch, and the mighty quoits ended up about eighteen inches high

10 Las Vegas (in *Viva Las Vegas*)

11 DA Pennebaker

12 Gary Busey

★ Wolfman Jack

TB Frank N Furter (*The Rocky Horror Picture Show*)

[40]
RIDLEY SCOTT

⑤ A *Blade Runner*

1 *1492: Conquest of Paradise*

2 'In space, no one can hear you scream'

3 (c)

4 It was a warning to stay away

5 In *Legend*

6 A four year life span

7 *Thelma and Louise*

8 Harvey Keitel

9 Rutger Hauer

10 Ripley (*Alien*) and Queen Isabella (*1492*)

11 An alien burst from his stomach

12 White (he was an android)

★ Sebastian made his best ever chess move

TB *The Duellists*

[41]

EWAN MCGREGOR

(5) Mark Renton

1 Playing the same character as a young man (Don Vito Corleone and Obi-Wan Kenobi respectively)

2 Anakin's exceptional aptitude for being a Jedi

3 *Lipstick on my Collar*

4 A *Shallow Grave*

5 He's afraid they'll attract attention to the stash of money Allen's corpse left them with

6 Angels, and they have to make McGregor and Cameron Diaz fall in love

7 Peter Greenaway

8 Liam Neeson and Barings

9 That Obi-Wan train Anakin to be a Jedi

10 Glam rock

11 Danny Boyle

12 He's a dentist, not a doctor, and he's brain-damaged (from where Cameron Diaz shot him in a William Tell-style stunt. You could also have jealousy.

★ *Kwaidan*

TB Opium suppositories (*Trainspotting*)

[42]
FILM AND TELEVISION

(S) Truman Burbank (Jim Carrey) himself

1 'Because it's neither rare nor well done.'

2 Tony Randall and Jack Klugman

3 Because films run at 24 frames a second, and TV and video at 25 frames a second (4.17% faster)

4 *ER*

5 Because of McCarthyist blacklisting

6 Hawkeye Pierce (in *M*A*S*H* on film and TV respectively)

7 Raymond Burr (*Rear Window* and *Ironside*)

8 From: Louis Hayward, Hugh Sinclair, George Sanders, Roger Moore, Ian Ogilvy and Val Kilmer

9 Robert Redford

10 Mark Renton (Ewan McGregor)

11 Paul Michael Glaser (*Starsky and Hutch* and *The Running Man*)

12 The Penguin (the *Batman* TV series and *Batman Returns*)

★ Billy Wilder

TB Heather O'Rourke (Carol Anne)

[43]
MARLON BRANDO

(5) *On the Waterfront*

1 The Actors' Studio
2 He had been paralysed
3 *Last Tango in Paris*
4 Because he was self-conscious about his ballooning weight
5 Made up as a Chinaman
6 Vivien Leigh
7 Frank Sinatra
8 'Whaddya got?'
9 Informing on Hollywood colleagues during the McCarthy witch-hunts
10 James Mason
11 Colonel Kurtz, based on the Kurtz of *Heart of Darkness*
12 *A Dry White Season*

★ Crawling, like a snail, along the edge of a straight razor, and surviving

TB In protest at the treatment of Native Americans

[44]
THE SILENT COMICS

(S) Charlie Chaplin

1   Fred Karno

2   Buster Keaton

3   A train (stolen from Keaton by union soldiers)

4   Custard-pie throwing

5   'Fatty' Arbuckle

6   About twenty minutes

7   Harold Lloyd

8   *Safety Last*

9   The Keystone Kops

10 Hal Roach

11 Edgar Kennedy

12 *The Battle of the Century*

★   Max Linder

TB It was silent (nearly ten years after the advent of sound)

[45]
EUROPEAN CINEMA

(S) In *Delicatessen*

1 Z

2 Home (Edgar Reitz's 1983 saga)

3 French (Veronique) and Polish (Veronika)

4 *Nikita (La Femme Nikita)*

5 It is psychic and can give flesh to remembered and longed-for people

6 He is a Jew (Solomon Perel) masquerading as an Aryan (based on real events)

7 Sweden (directed by Lasse Hallström, Jan Halldoff and Ingmar Bergman respectively)

8 The director himself

9 Hungary

10 Victoria Abril

11 *Come and See*

12 *Kanal*

★ It is the sewer system where fighters in the Warsaw Uprising of 1944 flee to

TB He is buried alive

[46]
JOHN FORD

(5) *The Grapes of Wrath*

1 *The Lost Patrol*

2 *The Searchers*

3 Tom Joad (Henry Fonda, in *The Grapes of Wrath*)

4 The Oklahoma Dustbowl

5 John Wayne

6 The IRA

7 *The Man Who Shot Liberty Valance*

8 (b)

9 *Stagecoach*

10 Henry Fonda

11 John Wayne and Jeffrey Hunter – they were looking for Wayne's niece
(Natalie Wood), who had survived an Indian raid on their relatives

12 Doc was a drunkard, Dallas a prostitute

★ *She Wore a Yellow Ribbon*

TB In *My Darling Clementine*

[47]
JAMES BOND

(**5**) Oddjob

1 His gun (a Beretta, to be swapped for a Walther)

2 SPECTRE

3 Naval Commander

4 King Zog

5 Winston Churchill

6 Big Ben chimed seven times at 6 o'clock

7 Felix Leiter

8 He tricks him into opening a briefcase booby-trapped with tear gas

9 Fortune-telling

10 Special Executive for Counterintelligence, Terrorism, Revenge and Extortion

11 Bono and The Edge of U2

12 Yaphet Kotto

★ Barry Nelson (in a 1954 TV adaptation of *Casino Royale*)

TB He had three nipples (*The Man with the Golden Gun*)

[48]

JAPANESE CINEMA

(5) *Seven Samurai*

1 *Rashomon*

2 A stylised theatrical tradition (strange to Western eyes, one of the influences which can make Japanese cinema seem so mysterious)

3 The disappointments of family life – an elderly couple visit their children, only to find them distant and uncommunicative

4 Kenji Mizoguchi

5 Kurosawa's *Yojimbo*

6 Anime

7 In Kurosawa's *Ikiru* (*Living*)

8 Toshiro Mifune

9 *Ran*

10 They are often exaggeratedly round and non-Japanese

11 Kon Ichikawa

12 *Hiroshima Mon Amour*

★ *Ugestu Monogatari*

TB Literally a Shadow Warrior, someone who donned their warlord's armour and mask and impersonated them in battle

[49]
CARY GRANT

(5) *North by Northwest*

1 Shirley Temple

2 Nazism

3 *Gunga Din*

4 A thief (*To Catch a Thief*)

5 Rosalind Russell

6 Bristol, as Archibald Leach

7 Wham (*Mr Blandings Builds his Dreamhouse* – it's an advertising slogan his maid came up with)

8 Randolph Scott

9 Mae West (*She Done Him Wrong*)

10 In *I Was a Male War Bride*

11 Hedda Hopper

12 Grace Kelly

★ *Philadelphia Story*

TB 'Old Cary Grant fine. How you?'

[50]
MODEL ANIMATION

(S) *The Magic Roundabout*

1   George Pal
2   *The Nightmare Before Christmas*
3   Aardman Animations
4   He sticks a rubber glove on his head and masquerades as a rooster
5   Jason (in *Jason and the Argonauts*)
6   Buster Keaton
7   Willis O'Brien
8   Bruno Shultz
9   Preston
10 Jan Svankmajer
11 Rex the Runt
12 Jiri Trnka

★   *The Comb*

TB Wensleydale

[51]
THAT EALING FEELING

(5) *The Lavender Hill Mob*

1   Michael Balcon

2   They were freed from rationing

3   Eight

4   Humouring the old dear's daydreams, they told her to keep it

5   He smashed a window and hid in a cupboard, escaping when his jailer went after the red herring

6   *The Titfield Thunderbolt*

7   *The Cruel Sea*

8   *Dead of Night*

9   He thinks he has discovered where he went wrong . . .

10 In *My Learned Friend*

11 *Whisky Galore*

12 John Mills

★   T. E. B. Clarke

TB *Let George Do It*

[52]
MUSIC FOR MOVIES

(S) They waltz

1 John Williams
2 The beginnings of the universe and the age of the dinosaurs
3 *Cabaret*
4 Vangelis (Papathanassiou)
5 A zither
6 Yes (played by a live orchestra or a pianist)
7 In *Dumbo*
8 Cole Porter
9 Bernard Herrmann
10 *Grease* (*Happy Days* and *American Graffiti* respectively)
11 Red, white and blue Minis (*The Italian Job*)
12 Woody Allen

★ Ronny Cox

TB Peter Gabriel

[53]
LAUREL AND HARDY

⑤ His tie

1 That it was over

2 Ollie had hit him over the head with a mallet

3 James Finlayson

4 Stan

5 *Two Tars*

6 A dog

7 Stan

8 In a French Foreign Legion fort (*Beau Chumps/Beau Hunks*)

9 They shared the same bed

10 *Brats*

11 Because their wives saw them on screen

12 A fake one made from materials they found to hand in the cabin

★ *Come Clean*

TB 'Yes, I never did.'

[54]

EDITING

(S) *Apocalypse Now*

1 Georges Méliès

2 A device that allows the editor to play and view the picture track in synchronisation with one or more soundtracks

3 The rectangle of light from Kane's bedroom

4 David Lean

5 A dissolve

6 Sergei Eisenstein

7 It will seem as if they are both looking in the same direction, which is likely to appear nonsensical

8 A strip at the start of a projection print showing a countdown

9 It was boldly cut even longer

10 They're outside the wrong house

11 'Noddy shots': footage of the interviewer supposedly reacting to the interviewee (who is probably no longer there)

12 Marking information onto the cutting copy

★ The viewers thought that the actor's expression changed in each sequence

TB George Lucas

[55]
BIBLICAL EPICS

(5) Charlton Heston

1 Samson (Victor Mature) talking about Delilah (Hedy Lamarr – in *Samson and Delilah*)

2 *Ben-Hur*

3 Rita Hayworth

4 There is a whiteout (a camera fault caused light to leak onto the film)

5 Judas Iscariot

6 King Herod

7 Otto Preminger

8 Groucho Marx

9 *Ben-Hur* (Charlton Heston)

10 Pharaoh Rameses

11 Peter Ustinov

12 David Bowie

★ Italian

TB Tod Browning

[56]
FRITZ LANG

⑤ Brigitte Helm

1 Peter Lorre's murderer
2 *The Woman in the Window*
3 By stabbing his attacker in the back with a pair of scissors
4 The heart
5 Cinemascope
6 'We'll decide who's Jewish!'
7 The Thousand Eyes of Dr Mabuse
8 *Fury*
9 Dorothy Parker
10 Bertolt Brecht
11 The need to avenge his fiancée's murder
12 A blind man recognises his whistling

★ *The Cabinet of Dr Caligari*

TB Siegfried (in *Die Nibelungen*)

[57]

HOLLYWOOD
AFTER *STAR WARS*

(S) *The Thing*

1 That it prompted an era of spectacle over content, juvenile effects-bonanzas over adult dramas

2 *Flash Gordon* (Topol and Timothy Dalton)

3 Cylons

4 An old Voyager space probe, part of its name obscured, embraced by an alien race as a mystical entity

5 *Seven Samurai*

6 (In the main) the first is an armature model, the second a computer-generated image

7 *Titanic*

8 Mark Hamill (in the *Batman* animated TV series)

9 *Tron*

10 Jeff Goldblum

11 The Ewoks

12 Lucas Arts

★ His uncle, Denis Lawson, played Wedge Antilles

TB *Howard the Duck: A New Breed of Hero*

[58]
CASABLANCA

S An airport
1 The Vichy régime
2 '. . . a hill of beans in this crazy world.'
3 Peter Lorre
4 Conrad Veidt
5 The papers of transit
6 Dooley Wilson
7 The Casablanca conference
8 Ronald Reagan
9 He was a wanted Resistance leader
10 Paris
11 Either *The Maltese Falcon* or *Passage to Marseilles*
12 As symbolic bars of the city they are imprisoned in
★ Warners
TB 'For the waters' (he was misinformed)

[59]
ROBERT DE NIRO

⑤ *Taxi Driver*

1 Martin Scorsese
2 With a baseball bat
3 Harvey Keitel
4 *Mean Streets*
5 The Devil (Lucifer) in *Angel Heart*
6 An airport heist (a Lufthansa consignment at Idlewild Airport)
7 In *The Godfather* and *The Godfather Part II*
8 In *Heat*
9 *Once Upon a Time in America*
10 Walken killed himself playing Russian Roulette
11 Method acting
12 *Awakenings*

★ Travis Bickle (in *Taxi Driver*)
TB Charles Grodin (in *Midnight Run*)

[60]

HAROLD LLOYD

(S) None

1 *Why Worry?*

2 By pulling a rotten tooth for him

3 *Safety Last*

4 His friend is supposed to climb the building but is dodging a policeman, and keeps promising to switch places with Lloyd between floors . . .

5 They were blown off by a real bomb mistakenly mixed in with prop bombs for a photo shoot

6 The Shriners (The Ancient Arabic Order of the Nobles of the Mystic Shrine)

7 *The Freshman*

8 *The Kid Brother*

9 Because his head is tucked under a metal bracket

10 It was completed as a silent, but with the arrival of sound several scenes were remade as sound scenes

11 Hal Roach

12 His sweetheart's marriage to a bigamist, in *Girl Shy*

★ Willie Work and Lonesome Luke

TB 1952

[61]

SERGEI EISENSTEIN

(S) The Odessa Steps sequence

1 Montage

2 Latvia

3 *Alexander Nevsky*

4 Edouard Tissé

5 *The General Line*

6 *Strike*

7 It is derived from the clash between adjacent shots, e.g. a cut from a crowd to a flock of sheep would suggest that the crowd was easily led. Just one shot or the other would not make this point

8 *Ivan the Terrible*

9 The Proletkult Theatre

10 *Que Viva Mexico* (or *Time in the Sun*)

11 True

12 The triumphal raised flag is tinted red

★ Grigori Alexandrov

TB Prokofiev

[62]
THE FRENCH NEW WAVE

(S) *Breathless*
 1 *Alphaville*
 2 *Jules et Jim*
 3 The director
 4 *Le Beau Serge*
 5 A mischievous girl causing mayhem in Paris
 6 Eric Rohmer
 7 *Au Revoir Les Enfants*
 8 A hit-and-run driver (Jean Yanne)
 9 *Cahiers du Cinéma*
10 *Last Year at Marienbad*
11 *Claire's Knee*
12 John Gielgud
 ★ Nicolas Roeg
TB The Angry Young Men

[63]

BETTE DAVIS

(5) *Now, Voyager*
1 *Jezebel*
2 Elizabeth I
3 *All About Eve*
4 *The Little Foxes*
5 Henry Fonda
6 Humphrey Bogart
7 George Sanders (Addison de Witt)
8 *Now, Voyager*
9 Errol Flynn
10 In *Dark Victory*
11 Cockney
12 Crawford
★ Ask a question and then duck
TB Laurence Olivier

[64]
THE RISE AND RISE OF HOLLYWOOD

(S) Nickelodeon

1 Edwin S. Porter

2 The Motion Picture Patents Company

3 New York

4 Continuity

5 Rin-Tin-Tin

6 The First World War

7 From: ancient Babylon, the time of Christ, the St Bartholomew's Day Massacre in France, and modern-day America

8 The studio practice of forcing exhibitors to show other, less desirable, films along with the blockbusters they really wanted

9 By the film industry itself

10 Its on-screen depiction of Christ

11 *Ben-Hur*

12 Sound film technology

★ Tinting colours the lighter areas, toning the darker

TB Buster Keaton

[65]

KIRK DOUGLAS

(5) The slave revolt led by *Spartacus*

1 A man trapped in a cave (Douglas delayed his rescue to boost the story value)

2 The bottle (*Gunfight at the OK Corral*)

3 (d) [(a) is Walter Matthau, (b) Herbert Lom and (c) Laurence Harvey]

4 The First World War

5 In *20,000 Leagues Under the Sea*

6 (b)

7 Harvey Keitel

8 Tony Curtis (*Spartacus* and *The Vikings*)

9 Boxing

10 A US general plotted a coup against a pacifist President he saw as a danger

11 *The Streets of San Francisco*

12 Robert Mitchum (*Out of the Past*)

★ He was the culprit's father

TB 'I was born poor'

[66]
PSYCHO

(S) The Bates Motel

1 She has stolen $40,000 from her workplace

2 To swap the Arizona plates she thinks conspicuous for California ones

3 Because he has a peephole view of it

4 Taxidermy (stuffing birds)

5 'His mother'

6 Loomis

7 He puts it in the trunk of her car, which he sinks in a lake

8 A combination of stabbing by Norman and falling down the stairs

9 Vera Miles

10 Norman desired her, and the mother element in his mind jealously removed a rival for his affections

11 The mummified remains of Norman's mother

12 Bernard Herrmann

★ Ed Gein

TB A skull is superimposed on it

[67]
WALT DISNEY

(S) *Aladdin*
1 *Dumbo*
2 Wart
3 The Beast of *Beauty and the Beast*
4 Mickey Mouse
5 Grumpy, Sleepy, Dopey, Doc, Bashful, Sneezy, Happy
6 Huey, Dewey and Louie
7 California, Florida, Japan and France
8 He was his conscience
9 *The Nightmare Before Christmas*
10 Elton John
11 *Fantasia*
12 Gargoyles
★ It manipulated the footage (speeded-up, reversed, etc.) for comic effect

TB Mortimer Mouse

[68]
THE DOCUMENTARY

(S) The Lumière brothers (Louis and Auguste)

1 Robert Flaherty
2 *The Civil War*
3 *Night Mail*
4 *Man with a Movie Camera*
5 *The Living Planet* and *The Trials of Life*
6 *Why We Fight*
7 John Grierson
8 Vietnam
9 The Turkestan–Siberia Railway (under construction)
10 Humphrey Jennings
11 *Civilisation*
12 John F. Kennedy and Hubert Humphrey

★ Fred Wiseman

TB Ed Murrow

[69]

GONE WITH THE WIND

(S) Atlanta

1   Louis B. Mayer

2   Margaret Mitchell

3   True

4   They had to de-emphasise the 'damn' to get it past the censors

5   Prissy (Butterfly McQueen)

6   A year

7   Errol Flynn

8   The Twelve Oaks barbecue

9   Leslie Howard

10 Victor Fleming, George Cukor and Sam Wood

11 Cukor

12 50 yards

★   Suellen O'Hara

TB There would always be Tara, the estate

[70]
BILLY WILDER

(S) Marilyn Monroe's

1 Peter Lorre
2 '. . . All right, Mr De Mille, I'm ready for my close-up'
3 By way of a four-day drinking binge
4 *The Seven Year Itch*
5 Buster Keaton
6 Austria
7 Cary Grant
8 George Raft
9 'Suggest handstand in shower'
10 *Double Indemnity*
11 Christine Vole (Marlene Dietrich)
12 *Schindler's List*

★ 'Thou shalt have right of final cut.'

TB Co-writer

[71]
SCIENCE FICTION

(5) Flash Gordon

1 Georges Méliès
2 He was an architect
3 *THX 1138* (directed by George Lucas)
4 *The Invisible Man*
5 *The Thing from Another World*
6 *Things to Come*
7 The crew of the Jupiter mission in *2001: A Space Odyssey*
8 *The Tempest*
9 The *Blade Runner* (Harrison Ford)
10 None – it was usually the camera that moved
11 *Invasion of the Body Snatchers*
12 Ellen Ripley (Sigourney Weaver) in *Alien*

★ *Solaris*

TB *The Day the Earth Stood Still*

[72]
WHO SAID ... ?

(S) Captain Willard (Martin Sheen) in *Apocalypse Now*

1 Ben Kenobi (Alec Guinness) in *Star Wars*

2 Dryden (Claude Rains) in *Lawrence of Arabia*

3 Laura (Celia Johnson) in *Brief Encounter*

4 Robin Hood (Errol Flynn) in *The Adventures of Robin Hood*

5 Charlie Croker (Michael Caine) in *The Italian Job*

6 Caspar Gutman (Sydney Greenstreet) in *The Maltese Falcon*

7 HAL (Douglas Rain) in *2001: A Space Odyssey*

8 Charles Foster Kane (Orson Welles) in *Citizen Kane*

9 Mr Blonde (Michael Madsen) in *Reservoir Dogs*

10 Roy Batty (Rutger Hauer) in *Blade Runner*

11 Dr Strangelove (Peter Sellers) in *Dr Strangelove*

12 Johnny Caspar (Jon Polito) in *Miller's Crossing*

★ Mike Connor (James Stewart) in *The Philadelphia Story*

TB E.T. in *E.T. The Extra-Terrestrial*

[73]
INGMAR BERGMAN

(5) Death

 1 Victor Sjöström
 2 Bibi Andersson
 3 The plague (or witch-hunts)
 4 Stephen Sondheim
 5 Chaplain to the Royal Family
 6 *Persona*
 7 *The Magic Lantern*
 8 *Brink of Life*
 9 *Fanny and Alexander*
10 He was arrested and charged with income tax fraud (the charges were later dropped)
11 *Hour of the Wolf*
12 Harriet Andersson or Ingrid Thulin respectively
 ★ Gunnar Fischer
TB *Through a Glass Darkly*

[74]
PULP FICTION

(S) Jules (Samuel L. Jackson)

1 Ezekiel

2 Butch's ass (i.e. he throws his fight in the fifth round)

3 'Ketchup'

4 To check how to correctly give an adrenaline shot to save Mia's (Uma Thurman's) life

5 Pumpkin and Honey Bunny

6 Mayonnaise

7 The Wolf (Harvey Keitel)

8 Because he gave Mia, his wife, a foot massage

9 He was meant to have a giant afro, but the wig never showed up

10 Vincent (John Travolta – because something bad always seems to happen when he does)

11 A pair of pliers and a blowtorch

12 The fact that the kid fired six shots at him and Vincent at point-blank range and missed every time

★ Knives

TB Either an Elvis person or a Beatles person

[75]
CLINT EASTWOOD

(5) *A Fistful of Dollars*

  1 *Rawhide*
  2 Sergio Leone
  3 *Play Misty for Me*
  4 The *High Plains Drifter*
  5 He was one of the secret servicemen who let JFK get shot
  6 Carmel
  7 None – he was The Man with No Name
  8 *Dirty Harry*
  9 To smoke out a group of traitors
 10 *The Outlaw Josey Wales*
 11 *Escape From Alcatraz*
 12 *Firefox*

  ★ He was faithful to his wife's memory, but didn't want her to think she repelled him

 TB His orang-utan buddy in *Every Which Way But Loose*, etc.

[76]
THE MARCH
OF TECHNOLOGY

(5) A speaker which produces low-frequency sounds (the deep bass sounds which for example make a home cinema system feel more like a real cinema)

1 George Eastman (of Eastman Kodak fame)

2 Because film at this time was shot at 16 frames per second. When played back at today's rate of 24 frames per second, they move 50% quicker than they should.

3 By releasing *The Jazz Singer*, and ushering in the sound era

4 The then very noisy cameras had to be incarcerated in soundproofed booths; actors' movements also tended to be restricted because they couldn't stray far from the primitive microphones

5 Technicolor

6 The former was highly unstable, and prone to degradation and catching fire

7 Between the sprocket-holes

8 The Steadicam

9 Betamax (about 15% better)

10 Vertical Helical Scanning (or Video Home System)

11 Computer-Generated Imagery

12 As a safeguard against global movie piracy (DVD poses such a threat because perfect copies of films can be made generation after generation)

★ It makes it possible to move the camera and the subject (e.g. a model spaceship) in precisely the same patterns again and again, making it easier to add layer after layer of elements to the shot.

TB It squeezes a widescreen image onto a standard frame of film (the process is reversed during projection)

[77]
HORROR

S Death's Head Moth pupae

1 *Nosferatu*

2 On *Halloween* and *Friday the 13th* respectively

3 Expressionist

4 George Romero

5 In *The Old Dark House*

6 *The Night of the Demon*

7 Linda Blair

8 (a) [(b) is *Whatever Happened to Mary Jane*, and (c) is *A Short Film About Love*]

9 Dario Argento

10 *Bride of Frankenstein*

11 *A Nightmare on Elm Street*

12 Bela Lugosi

★ *The Golem*

TB David Cronenberg

[78]
THE STUDIO SYSTEM

(S) From: Charlie Chaplin, Mary Pickford, D. W. Griffith and Douglas Fairbanks

1 MGM

2 Radio-Keith-Orpheum

3 From: MGM, 20th Century Fox, Warner Bros, Paramount and RKO

4 From: Columbia, Universal and United Artists

5 Universal

6 Screwball comedy

7 20th Century Fox

8 Their theatre chains

9 Television

10 The drive-in

11 RKO

12 Coca-Cola

★ One which controls the production *and* distribution of its films (giving it more overall control than a mere producer)

TB King Vidor's *The Big Parade* (1925)

[79]
GEORGE LUCAS

(S) *Star Wars*

1 Modesto

2 He nearly died when he wrapped his Fiat Bianchina round a tree

3 *American Graffiti*

4 *Carrie*

5 Dolby Stereo

6 She was Marcia Griffin, later to become Mrs Lucas

7 By hitting him with a hammer

8 The University of Southern California

9 Because Hamill had just gone through the windscreen of his car and lacerated his face

10 Industrial Light and Magic

11 Because he had passed on the stress of directing to Steven Spielberg

12 THX

★ To provide Greedo's dialogue

TB Francis Ford Coppola

[80]
SCREENWRITING

(S) Harrison Ford to George Lucas

1 Writer Robert Bolt had been jailed after a CND protest, and refused to sign the statements of good behaviour needed for his release – until Spiegel talked him into it

2 Thomas More

3 *Chariots of Fire*

4 It advises the actor to pause for a moment for comic effect

5 *The Grapes of Wrath*

6 *M*A*S*H* – Lardner scripted the original feature, and Gelbart presided over the TV series

7 *Glengarry Glen Ross* – David Mamet

8 A Medium Close-Up shot

9 *Barton Fink* (John Turturro)

10 Ben Hecht

11 Herman Mankiewicz

12 Joe Eszterhas

★ A Master Scene Script reads rather like a stage play, but a Shooting Script is broken down into individual shots

TB It was a pseudonym for the McCarthy-blacklisted writer Dalton Trumbo

[81]
THE OSCARS

(**S**) Walt Disney (26 – the company has since won more)

1 The part that holds his brains is sliced off

2 Tatum O'Neal in *Paper Moon*

3 Jessica Tandy in *Driving Miss Daisy*

4 Marlon Brando (Best Actor) in *The Godfather* and Robert de Niro (Best Supporting Actor) in *The Godfather Part II* – both playing Vito Corleone

5 Hattie McDaniel (Best Supporting Actress) in *Gone with the Wind*

6 The Hustons (Walter: Best Supporting Actor in *Treasure of the Sierra Madre*; John: Best Director and Adapted Screenplay in the same; Anjelica: Best Supporting Actress in *Prizzi's Honor*)

7 From: *Cimarron, Dances with Wolves* and *Unforgiven*

8 Laurence Olivier (in *Hamlet*)

9 Katharine Hepburn (she won four)

10 Woody Allen (with 13 Screenplay nominations)

11 *Coming Home*

12 Linda Hunt (Billy Kwan) in *The Year of Living Dangerously*

★ Harold Russell, a disabled war veteran, for *The Best Years of Our Lives* (Best Supporting Actor and a Special Oscar for 'bringing hope and courage to his fellow veterans')

TB Lionel Barrymore (*A Free Soul*) and Ethel Barrymore (*None but the Lonely Heart*)

[82]
SATYAJIT RAY

(5) A train
 1 Cannes
 2 Song of the Little Road
 3 Calcutta
 4 Jean Renoir
 5 Bengali
 6 Ibsen
 7 *Aparajito (The Unvanquished)* and *The World of Apu*
 8 The British are manoeuvring for control of their home state
 9 *Bicycle Thieves*
10 In childbirth
11 *The Visitor*
12 Ravi Shankar

 ★ *Mahanagar (The Big City)* and *Charulata (The Lonely Wife)*

TB From a fever caught by dancing in the rain

[83]
VIETNAM MOVIES

(5) Colonel Kilgore (Robert Duvall, in *Apocalypse Now*)

1   *Hamburger Hill*

2   *Platoon, Born on the Fourth of July* and *Heaven and Earth*

3   Tom Cruise

4   *The Green Berets*

5   He shot his Sergeant (Lee Ermey), and then himself. (The title refers to a bullet's casing)

6   John Cazale

7   *Coming Home*

8   Willem Dafoe and Tom Berenger

9   Russian Roulette

10 *Rambo* (and, of course, *Rambo III*)

11 *Go Tell the Spartans*

12 The ritual slaughter of a cow

★   American troops massacred villagers

TB He thought he was a bird (*Birdy*)

[84]
CITIZEN KANE

(**5**) The meaning of Kane's dying word, 'Rosebud'

1 *That he'll do all he can*

2 'You can take my word for it, there will be no war'

3 Opera

4 Xanadu

5 *The March of Time*

6 The Colorado Lode goldmine

7 Herman J. Mankiewicz

8 He was covered in mud, and she had toothache

9 *The New York Daily Inquirer*

10 'Rosebud', and the idea that it could explain everything about a human being (a McGuffin is a red herring)

11 John Houseman (who fell out with Welles)

12 He completed it in like manner

★ German Expressionism

TB Charles Foster

[85]
STANLEY KUBRICK

(S) *Dr Strangelove*

1 A photograph, to *Look* Magazine

2 *Fear and Desire* (1953)

3 A scene in *A Clockwork Orange*, where his character is being visually brainwashed, required his eyelid to be clamped open

4 *Spartacus* (Kirk Douglas)

5 *Full Metal Jacket*

6 *Lolita* (Sue Lyon)

7 *The Killing*

8 HAL (*2001: A Space Odyssey*)

9 He was impotent, and blamed it on fiendish Russian water fluoridators

10 *Barry Lyndon*

11 He was possessed by the murderous spirit of the previous caretaker

12 To have acquitted three soldiers accused of cowardice

★ Laurence Olivier and Tony Curtis

TB Major Kong (Slim Pickens)

[86]
THE GANGSTER MOVIE

(S) *The Godfather* (Don Vito Corleone)

1 Warner Brothers

2 A grapefruit

3 A Treasury Official

4 At *Miller's Crossing*

5 Albert Finney (Leo)

6 Humphrey Bogart, James Cagney and Edward G. Robinson

7 Paul Muni and Al Pacino

8 Faye Dunaway and Madonna

9 To disillusion the Dead End Kids of gangster glamour

10 Al Capone

11 Jewish

12 *Goodfellas*

★ (a) [(b) is *Miller's Crossing*, and (c) *The Roaring Twenties*]

TB James Cagney at the climax of *White Heat*

[87]

LAWRENCE OF ARABIA

(5) *Not minding* that it hurt

1 As a side-show of a side-show

2 The heavy Turkish guns were pointed the other way, against sea attack, and could not be turned around

3 Colonel Brighton (Anthony Quayle)

4 Robert Bolt

5 One drowned in a quicksand; the other was crippled when a detonator went off in his clothing, and Lawrence had to shoot him to prevent him being captured and tortured

6 Omar Sharif (as Sherif Ali – he was defending his well)

7 Slapped him in the face

8 Because that would give them military muscle, and independence

9 Lawrence executed him: justice was done by a neutral

10 Amid the wreckage of the Turkish train he had blown up

11 'I enjoyed it'

12 In a motorcycle crash in England

★ To suggest that it was his pleasure

TB General Murray

[88]

JAMES STEWART

⑤ A six-foot invisible rabbit (as hallucinated by drunkard Elwood P. Dowd)

1 *Mr Smith Goes to Washington*

2 Tracy Lord (Katharine Hepburn)

3 Henry Fonda

4 A bomber squadron

5 He's an angel

6 The floor parts and they fall into the swimming pool beneath

7 By dazzling him with his camera flashgun

8 Cochise

9 By shooting him in the hand

10 Lionel Barrymore

11 At a Sunday church service

12 By skipping town without paying his fee

★ The Leopold–Loeb case of the 1920s, where two bored young men committed a murder for kicks

TB Indiana

[89]
CLARK GABLE

(5) Rhett Butler (in *Gone with the Wind*)

1 The San Francisco Earthquake
2 He's a reporter looking for a story
3 Fletcher Christian
4 'Square John' Sand (Spencer Tracy)
5 Marilyn Monroe (in *The Misfits* – Gable had a fatal heart attack shortly after)
6 *Mogambo*
7 $120,000
8 '. . . they all like him.'
9 Carole Lombard
10 *Red Dust*
11 Joan Crawford
12 *Comrade X*

★ Irving Thalberg

TB Milton Berle

[90]
QUENTIN TARANTINO

(5) A Royale

1 Stealer Wheel's *Stuck in the Middle with You*

2 We don't (the camera pans away and we only hear it)

3 Elmore Leonard's

4 He had gone to the toilet

5 Steve Buscemi's Mr Pink

6 The script

7 Pam Grier

8 Tim Roth

9 Samuel L. Jackson

10 We never find out (*Pulp Fiction*)

11 Mr Pink sounded like Mr Faggot, Mr Brown like Mr Turd

12 Because vampires are on the loose

★ Hopper suggests that Sicilians have black (Moorish) blood in their veins

TB Harvey Keitel

[91]
JAMES CAMERON

(**S**) *That* diamond around her neck

1   Ripley and the alien queen, in *Aliens*
2   Because they were computer-generated
3   There's no foam breaking at their bases to make them easier to see
4   A traitor (Carter Burke) had released the larvae
5   A killer epidemic
6   The T1000 was frozen by liquid nitrogen from another tanker (and shattered)
7   By slicing off his hand to reveal his cyberskeleton
8   Michael Biehn
9   He stands at the sinking bridge until the windows implode, and so drowns
10 By threatening to incinerate her eggs with a flame-thrower
11 *Ben Hur*
12 Breathing a special oxygenated fluid (we breathe fluid in the womb)
★   Two (he was working his way through the phone directory)
TB By crushing its head in an industrial press

[92]
INGRID BERGMAN

⑤ Cary Grant (Agent Devlin)

1 Intermezzo

2 Golda Meir (in the TV movie A Woman Named Golda)

3 David O. Selznick

4 For Whom the Bell Tolls

5 A-Bomb uranium

6 Roberto Rossellini

7 Garbo

8 Lund and Lazlo

9 Joan of Arc

10 Salvador Dali, for Spellbound (it didn't happen, of course)

11 Drive her mad

12 From: Gaslight, Anastasia and Murder on the Orient Express

★ Lithuania

TB Autumn Sonata

[93]
BRITISH FILM

(5) *The Third Man*

1 Will Hay

2 Alfred Hitchcock

3 By casting it as souvenir Eiffel Towers

4 *The Knack*

5 Alexander Korda

6 The Holy Grail (*Monty Python and the Holy Grail*)

7 The apparently everlasting suit fell apart, so safeguarding the jobs of textile workers

8 *Trainspotting*

9 Michael Powell and Emeric Pressburger

10 Hammer Studios

11 *Henry V*

12 *The Ladykillers*

★ Poland, Hungary and Lithuania

TB James Mason

[94]
SEAN CONNERY

(S) Alcatraz

1   Coffins

2   *Hell Drivers*

3   From: Eric Pohlmann (*From Russia with Love* and *Thunderball*),
    Anthony Dawson (*From Russia with Love*), Donald Pleasance (*You
    Only Live Twice*), Charles Gray (*Diamonds are Forever*) and Max von
    Sydow (*Never Say Never Again*)

4   Goldfinger's Kentucky stud farm

5   At the Mr Universe contest

6   *The Name of the Rose*

7   Pretending the corpse was still alive, he shot it to terrorise the man into
    confessing

8   Indiana Jones (Harrison Ford, in *Indiana Jones and the Last Crusade*)

9   *Outland*

10 The voice of the dragon

11 From filming the golf scenes in *Goldfinger*

12 George Lazenby (*On Her Majesty's Secret Service*), David Niven
    (*Casino Royale*), and Connery himself (*You Only Live Twice*)

★   He has appeared in Robin Hood films where they have played Marian
    (he was Robin in *Robin and Marian*, with Hepburn, and King Richard
    in *Robin Hood: Prince of Thieves*, with Mastrantonio)

TB *Trainspotting*

[95]
ASIAN CINEMA

(S) Noodles
 1 Quentin Tarantino
 2 Tollywood
 3 Japan
 4 Israel
 5 *Red Sorghum*
 6 South Korea
 7 Madras
 8 Saddam Hussein
 9 *Salaam Bombay!*
10 *In the Realm of the Senses*
11 Chow Yun-Fat
12 The Japanese occupation of China

 ★ To get a bead on the exact position where the besieging commander
    will be sitting after dark

TB Bruce Lee

[96]
FILM ACTING

(5) Daniel Day-Lewis

1   Lee Strasberg

2   The Method

3   Sherlock Holmes

4   *Casablanca*

5   Laurence Olivier

6   Michael Caine's

7   John Wayne (Marion Morrison was his real name)

8   The Barrymores

9   Katharine Hepburn (*Morning Glory, Guess Who's Coming to Dinner, The Lion in Winter* and *On Golden Pond*)

10 Shirley Temple

11 Moira Shearer

12 Lon Chaney

★   Mime artist Marcel Marceau

TB 'Actors should be treated like cattle'

[97]
DAVID LEAN

(5) *Lawrence of Arabia*

1 Editing

2 The notorious Burma Railway

3 *Ryan's Daughter*

4 *Oliver Twist*

5 Magwitch (*Great Expectations*)

6 She and her cobweb-laden room were set alight by a candle

7 *Nostromo*

8 Julie Christie (Lara)

9 (c)

10 Fagin and Bill Sykes respectively

11 Noël Coward

12 A *Brief Encounter*

★ Michael Powell

TB *The Sound Barrier*

[98]
THE COEN BROTHERS

(5) *Miller's Crossing*

1   The hula-hoop (*The Hudsucker Proxy*)
2   *Barton Fink*
3   'Danny Boy'
4   Minnesota
5   John Turturro
6   She's a cop and he's a crook
7   She's pregnant
8   M. Emmett Walsh
9   Joel and Ethan respectively
10 By running down the boardroom table and throwing himself out of the window
11 Jeff Bridges
12 Swedish
★   Dashiell Hammett
TB The moment is docked from their pay

[99]
FILM NOIR

(S) Because of a hurricane

1 He directed the former, and played the villain in the latter

2 Twice (the first time as *Satan Met a Lady*)

3 *Kiss of Death*

4 Brains

5 *Blade Runner*

6 A high contrast scheme of stark light and mysterious shadow (e.g. the slatted light from a venetian blind)

7 *Boomerang*

8 Fred MacMurray

9 Sydney Greenstreet's Fat Man (Caspar Gutman)

10 He was Walter Huston, his father

11 *Dead Men Don't Wear Plaid*

12 Bogart to Mary Astor

★ The criminal underworld (fearful of the harm he was doing to their image)

TB In colour, and with a happy ending

[100]

THE GODFATHER

(5) Mario Puzo

1   Finding the severed head of his prize horse in his bed

2   Irish-German

3   None

4   Sergio Leone

5   John Cazale

6   World War II

7   On a lake

8   Luca Brasi

9   Sofia Coppola

10   Nino Rota

11   Best Adapted Screenplay

12   She is killed by a car bomb

★   His bullet-proof vest wrapped around a fish

TB   Richard Conte (the others are respectively his sister and nephews)

[101]
BUSTER KEATON

⑤ Stone Face

1 Harry Houdini

2 Roscoe (Fatty) Arbuckle

3 The escalator (which jammed his foot at the top, then threw him clear to the floor ten feet below)

4 The Canfields have a long-running feud with him, but the rules of Southern hospitality forbid them harming a guest in their home

5 The Chaplin studio

6 It was the only time he used a stuntman (an Olympic pole-vault champion)

7 *The General*

8 The track curves, and the blast passes to one side

9 False: it is a pursuing Union train

10 Charlie Chaplin

11 *The Navigator*

12 50%

★ A waterspout forced his neck against the railroad track

TB *Intolerance*

[102]
JODIE FOSTER

(5) Signals from outer space

1 Coppertan sun tan lotion

2 Disney

3 *Taxi Driver*

4 Shooting President Reagan

5 White trash West Virginia

6 Susan Sarandon (for *Thelma and Louise*)

7 The gang-rape of Charlene (Foster)

8 *Alice Doesn't Live Here Anymore*

9 *Bugsy Malone*

10 Japan

11 *Little Man Tate*

12 Richard Gere, following Gérard Depardieu in *The Return of Martin Guerre*

★ Yale

TB Michelle Pfeiffer

[103]

SHAKESPEARE
IN THE MOVIES

⑤ Leo DiCaprio and Claire Danes

1 *The Taming of the Shrew*
2 A fascist 1930s Britain
3 He turns round, rubs his hands together and spits on the floor
4 *Romeo and Ethel, the Pirate's Daughter*
5 They were played by brothers Joseph and Ralph Fiennes respectively
6 Robbie the Robot
7 *Rosencrantz and Guildenstern are Dead*
8 The Jets and Sharks gangs
9 They have become sons
10 For 'displaying a female on the public stage'
11 Christopher (Kit) Marlowe
12 *Henry V*

★ *The Tempest*

TB The double suicide of Romeo and Juliet

[104]

LEONARDO DICAPRIO

⑤ A fish tank

1 The unborn Leo kicked his mother while she was looking at a Leonardo da Vinci painting in the Uffizi

2 *Lassie*

3 Robert De Niro

4 Japan

5 Jeremy Irons, John Malkovich, Gérard Depardieu and Gabriel Byrne

6 *The Basketball Diaries*

7 Johnny Depp (*What's Eating Gilbert Grape?*)

8 Mark Wahlberg (Marky Mark)

9 Fifteen

10 *Boogie Nights*

11 He died of heroin-induced heart failure (*The Basketball Diaries* being about heroin addiction)

12 *Strictly Ballroom*

★ Arthur Rimbaud

TB *Celebrity*

[105]
FADE OUT

⑤ *A Bug's Life*

1 *Casablanca*

2 *Heaven Can Wait*

3 *The Usual Suspects*

4 *The African Queen*

5 *Lawrence of Arabia*

6 *King Kong*

7 *The Good Earth*

8 *Desperate Journey*

9 *Pulp Fiction*

10 *Citizen Kane*

11 James Mason

12 Stanley Kubrick

★ Jean Renoir

TB *The Player*

Halliwell's Film & Video Guide
2001 Edition

EDITED BY JOHN WALKER

'Heavy enough to be authoritative, light enough to be idiosyncratic'
The Times

The 2001 edition of *Halliwell's Film & Video Guide* is perennially
entertaining, comprehensive and indispensable. The best known of
British film guides, *Halliwell's* is the undisputed bible for film
enthusiasts and trivia buffs – a must-have for every movie-goer. Fully
revised and updated to include hundreds of new films, it is packed
full with cast and credit information and pithy comment.
It also includes:

★ Plot synopses and critical evaluations; video cassette, laser disc
and DVD availability; quotes from contemporary reviews;
alternative titles and original publicity tags

★ Easy-to-follow icons denoting films suitable for family viewing,
Academy Award winners and nominees, soundtrack availability,
computer-coloured versions and video format compatibility

★ Lists of four-star and three-star films by title and year, and a list of
all the Academy Award winners for best picture and director, best
actor and actress, best supporting actor and actress, and best original
and adapted screenplays

£19.99
0 00 653219 5
Publication: 2 October 2000